In Art As in Life

A History of Beauty and a Critique of
Postmodern Relativism

Ilario Colli

Fulton Books, Inc.
Meadville, PA

Published by Fulton Books 2021

ISBN 978-1-64654-967-2 (paperback)
ISBN 978-1-64654-968-9 (digital)

Printed in the United States of America

In Art as in Life

"In Art as in Life *would represent a major achievement for any writer. It contains numerous ideas of genuine originality, the likes of which we rarely come across.*
I believe it will prove a real contribution to the wider understanding of our culture."

—Robert Gibbs, former publisher, *Limelight Magazine*

"*Colli has an outstanding and probing intellect...He has an exceptional command of language.*"

—Victoria Rogers, Associate Professor in Musicology,
University of Western Australia, School of Music

"*I can see that Colli is a master of English language communication. He ought, quite clearly, to be Australia's leading classical music critic.*"

—Robert Matthew-Walker, Editor, Musical Opinion

"In Art as in Life *represents a stimulating work-out for the mind of the creative artist as well as students of thought and culture.*"

—Nicholas Bannan, Associate Professor of Music,
University of Western Australia, School of Music

Contents

Introduction

The common truism, "Art imitates life," runs deeper than we usually think, and those who use it flippantly utter a truth much deeper than they realise. The aesthetic values informing the creation of art in any given era form a relationship so intimately symbiotic with the metaphysical values running chronologically alongside them, that, with practically no exceptions, the history of Western arts has seen a perfectly parallel evolution of the two, with all major metaphysical developments producing—with a delay of, at most, several generations—directly correspondent alterations in the manner and spirit in which art is delivered, received, and signified.

In the current age, this symbiotic relationship is as strong and palpable as ever, and its effects as all-encompassing. The contemporary moral climate in the West can, without exaggeration, be described as one of near total relativism. A thinly disguised cognate of nihilism, which is its immediate forebear, relativism posits that, since there are no universal values, no eternal and immutable Truth, each truth is as valid as the next, and consequently no moral system can hold supremacy over another.

The historical forces that led to this present position were relentless and inexorable and have yielded an equivalent spirit of relativism governing the conception of art, which in academic circles goes by the name *Postmodernism.* Like its ethical counterpart, Postmodernism argues in the ultimate absurdity of absolute ideals. Art can provide no window into the Truth, because Truth doesn't exist, and any attempt to capture it is, at best, misguided, and at worst, obtuse and heretical. Beauty—that highest and noblest of human truths, which until the early twentieth century, it was the primary objective of Western Art to humbly serve and glorify—is now a concept blurred and diluted. In the name of a self-deceiving confusion of ideas that parades itself as anti-dogmatism, what is universal is universally denied and what is noble is routinely confused with what is base and ugly. The artist—who, though often innovative within the restricted confines of his form, has in all eras been a hapless slave to the thought currents outside it—gleefully buys into this self-deception, producing Art that makes a mockery of the noble. The artist who, status quo notwithstanding, sets about using his form to convey universal Truth and Beauty, puts himself at odds with the establishment and at risk of critical derision.

With the following piece, I attempt to illustrate that the contemporary postmodern aesthetic, like the moral relativism that spawned it, is *not*—as it's often claimed to be—a sign of a robust, self-confident, creative culture, but rather, the primary artistic symptom of a metaphysically ailing civilisation, one still recovering from the demise of moral absolutism and still struggling to find meaning in its wake.

Part I: A History of Beauty

The Middle Ages

Before the advent of twentieth-century Postmodernism, Beauty was not a flexible concept. It was neither easily amenable to change nor susceptible to individual quibbles regarding its fundamental nature and purpose. It was incontestable as a fixed quantity, though not necessarily agreed upon unanimously in its details. It was employed almost uninterruptedly as the guiding aesthetic principle in the creation of Western Art from the days of its medieval infancy. Beauty, as it was conveyed through the artistic medium, was invariably put to use in the service of that one, supreme governing principle; that value of all values, eternal and immutable, the *ideal* par excellence, which itself legitimated Beauty, and rendered meaningful all attempts to pursue it: god.[1]

In the medieval conception, man, though created in god's image, partook of none of his divine energy. He and god stood at opposite ends of the cosmic spectrum. While man was firmly planted on earth, god dwelt far above him, in heavenly realms remote and inaccessible. A helpless creature who rarely lived beyond fifty and was constantly threatened by illness and other scourges,[2] man could do no better, in this life, than submit himself to the divine will and

---

[1] 'God' is, in this essay, intentionally rendered with a lower case initial unless reported in a quote by another author in whose writing it was originally capitalized. This is done to reflect the beliefs of the writer.

[2] For a depiction of the squalor of medieval life, see Bertrand Russell's *A History of Western Philosophy*, p. 286.

could expect to have no more decisive a hand in his own destiny than that granted him by god through prayer.

In his *City of God,* St. Augustine (AD 354–AD 430), arguably the most influential medieval theologian, divides the cosmos into two distinct realms that have more than a hint of Platonism about them: the City of Man and the City of God. These two cities, Augustine argues, were "formed by two different forms of love"—the former by the sinful "love of self, even to the contempt of god," the latter by the "love of god, even to the contempt of self."[3] Though the meaning Augustine assigns to his two cities shift about throughout the work, a literal interpretation is readily available. The City of God is the ideal Christian utopia, a society whose inhabitants place god first before each other and even themselves; a city governed by *Caritas* or a pure and selfless love for god. The City of Man, on the other hand, is one overrun by sin and vice; one whose inhabitants put their base, selfish needs first and live their lives, not "according to the spirit," but "according to the flesh."[4] Augustine's point is this: if we are to achieve salvation, we need to act, in this life, like an ideal citizen of the City of God, avoiding all sins of the flesh and directing our attention away from affairs of this world toward those of the next.

In the major philosophical works of the period, there are a number of similarly human-effacing themes. The most important, perhaps, is the limitation of man's reason and his consequent reliance on god's Truth for salvation. For St. Augustine[5] and St. Thomas Aquinas (1225–1274),[6] man's innate faculties for independent reasoning were, at best, flawed and, at worst, spiritually deadly.[7] To follow one's

---

3 Book XIV.

4 Ibid.: "Because some live according to the flesh and others according to the spirit there have arisen two diverse and conflicting cities..."

5 *City of God,* Book XI: "But since the mind itself, though naturally capable of reason and intelligence, is disabled by besotting and inveterate vices...it had, in the first place, to be impregnated with faith, and so purified."

6 *Summa contra Gentiles,* Book 1.3: "The Intellect is Incapable of Contemplating Divine Substance"

7 *Summa Theologica,* Of the Act of Faith: "Since man's nature is dependent on a higher nature, natural knowledge does not suffice for its perfection, and some supernatural knowledge is necessary..."

own inner logic while ignoring one's faith was to lead oneself into falsehood and, if one was especially misguided, to damnation.

The story of Adam's fall served as the ultimate cautionary tale against the perils of depending on human reason. In the Garden of Eden, god had given Adam and Eve everything they could possibly need: peace, happiness, companionship, and his constant love and protection. All they had to do in order to remain in this blissful state was to abstain from eating the fruit of the tellingly named tree of knowledge. The fruit, here, represented the pernicious lure of free thought and scientific curiosity, which god deemed unnecessary—after all, in a perfect, divinely ordered world, where faith rules supreme and all questions have preconfigured, divine answers, what need could there be for independent inquiry? By plucking the forbidden fruit, they sent god a clearly defiant message: that his divine utopia wasn't enough for them; that faith wasn't enough for them; that *god* wasn't enough for them. They needed more. They needed to *learn,* to navigate through the world on their own terms, with their own "flawed" human faculties. They had perpetrated the ultimate act of rebellion against faith and had to be ejected forthwith.

Of equal importance to faith, in medieval epistemology, was the concept of the *Logos*. First proposed by the pre-Socratic philosopher, Heraclitus (c. 535–c. 475 BCE), for whom it meant something akin to the cosmos's overarching ordering principle, the term was appropriated by second-century theologians Justin Martyr (AD 100–AD 165) and Origen (c. 185–c. 254), in whose hands it took on a distinctly Christian meaning. Reading the enigmatic gospel of John, these early church thinkers had found several rather vexing references to the word "word" (one of *Logos's* myriad translations into English):

> "In the beginning, there was the Word...
> And the Word became flesh and made his dwelling among us, and we saw his glory, the glory as of the Father's only Son..."[8]

---

[8] John 1:1–15

Not knowing, at first, what to make of a mysterious, shape-shifting "word" (*Logos*) that could live among men, the theologians plundered Greek thought and set about marrying it to Christian theology. They deduced—logically enough—that John's *Logos* could be no other than Heraclitus's divine ordering principle embodied in the form of the Christ. Christ *was* the *Logos*; that thing by which all was understood and without which nothing could be.

The *Logos* would become a central Christian dogma, with all major medieval thinkers—Augustine, John Scotus (AD 815–AD 977), Bonaventure (1221–1274), and Aquinas, to name a few—reasserting it in one way or another. In the hands of the Christians, the *Logos* took on the significance of "ultimate cosmic intermediary." If man's faculties were flawed and limited, if he was bereft of the divine spark and of any direct portal into the realm of divine truth, the *Logos* would provide it. The *Logos* is the "light that shines in the darkness";[9] that which illuminates man's idle and ignorant mind with god's divine ideas. For the Greeks, the *Logos* had been an ontological principle defining the basic structure of being. For the Christians, it acquired an epistemological function. The *Logos* was, not only *in* everything, but the way *to* everything. It was the way to understand the divine mind; the one and only path to truth.

In Art as in life, medieval man was burdened by innate intellectual and spiritual shortcomings, and ever dependent on the divine for inspiration. Most notable works of twelfth and thirteenth-century art—from the Gothic cathedrals of Reims and Chartres to Pérotin's sacred chants to the mosaics of Cimabue—were conceived to reflect man's subservient role in god's cosmic game. There was little room here, for individual whim, for human artifice. The artist's job was to capture the beauty of the divine, of the all-pervasive *Logos,* not to indulge an inner impulse for creative self-expression. Her ego took back seat to the duty she served and the artistic license was foregone in favour of the aesthetic certainty afforded by clear and straightforward stylistic guidelines. If, on the odd occasion, she managed to pull off a feat of creative brilliance, credit would inevitably go not to her, but to

---

[9] Gospel of John 1:1–15

god. She hadn't had a moment of purely human inspiration, no. The light of god's *Logos* had rather illuminated her, momentarily opened a portal to the divine into which she'd had the blessing to briefly peer.

In Art as in the medieval cosmos at large, god held dominion over man; thus, subject matter triumphed over the form and style with which it was represented, yielding an Art stripped of all manneristic indulgences. In Pérotin's "Viderunt Omnes" (1198)—a reworking of an older Gregorian chant in an emerging style of polyphony known as organum—a fundamental remains fixed and unmoving in the bass, like the all-permeating *Logos* itself. Above it, the higher voices of saints and angels weave a sparse and austere filigree, often bumping into each other at dissonant intervals and coming to rest only at bare, lifeless harmonic fourths and fifths.

Santa Trinita Maestà (Cimabue, 1290)

Some ninety years later, the world would see a pictorial rendering of the same cosmic distribution in Cimabue's *Santa Trinità Maestà* (1290). Here, the Virgin Mary is portrayed holding the infant Jesus. She sits squarely in the centre on her celestial throne, flanked on three sides by angels and prophets. It's a two-dimensional depiction, lacking all depth and perspective. Its protagonists are dry and lifeless with vacuous facial expressions and limbs twisted at unnatural angles. Their position-ing around the virgin with child is highly figurative, representing, not physically reality, but the strict hierarchical order of the heavenly realm.

In the literature of the Middle Ages, we see an equivalent god-maximising and human-diminishing tendency. Man's toils and triumphs are, of course, represented, but oftentimes indirectly, with allegorical devices whose purpose it is to lift the narrative above the terrestrial plain and into the divine. Insights into human nature lack psychological subtlety and characters are often of the stock variety, privy of nuance and three-dimensionality. Love is depicted according to the Augustinian model: privy of sinful indulgences of the flesh. In great medieval romances such as the twelfth-century *Lancelot* and the fourteenth-century *Sir Gewain and the Green Knight*, human love, in all its foibles, is often replaced by its more celestial courtly equivalent: the "pure" love of a valiant knight for a woman of high social stand-ing and impeccable moral character, whom he admires from afar but never soils with his touch. In Dante's *Divine Comedy* (1308–1320), arguably the greatest medieval epic, the hero's journey is represented symbolically as a pilgrim's ascent from hell to *empyrean*, the highest circle of heaven. When he finally sees his beloved, Beatrice, she is adorned in a "cloud of flowers,"[10] appearing more a heavenly ideal than a flesh-and-blood woman. Rather than rushing to embrace him, she acts like a divine arbiter, reprimanding him for his human frailties.[11]

In the *Trinità* and "*Viderunt,*" as in the medieval epics, the aes-thetic message is the same: Art is no place for man's caprices or for an overindulgent exploration of the human condition. If man is frail, limited, and entirely dependent on divine light for his spiritual nour-ishment, it must be deemed necessary for him to limit his creative task to bow in deference to it. If the realm of man was chaotic, unpre-dictable and full of sin, one could find solace from it in the solid moral logic of god's firmament. Here, the all-knowing and all-pow-erful *Logos* sat on its Cimabuan throne, its constant cosmic energy

---

[10] Purgatorio, Canto: XXX

[11] Ibid.: "He turned his steps aside from the True Way | pursuing the false images of good | that promise what they never wholly pay"

humming outwards in all directions, like Pérotin's fundamental, pervading the fabric of all things and bestowing order and meaning. Beauty, for the medieval artist, was precisely this: the inescapable, absolute metaphysical truth of the divine *logos*.

The Renaissance

In the late fourteenth and fifteenth centuries, there began to be felt in Europe, a shift in our way of seeing the world so far-reaching in its implications, that it has since been deemed as marking the dawn of modernity.[12] It is known by the name *Renaissance* or "rebirth." In Italian city states like Florence, wealth and culture, a notable freedom on the municipal level and a relative separateness of church from state[13] led to a moral climate in which man was free to mature an unprecedented confidence in his own capabilities. It was the era of voracious polymaths; *uomini universali,*[14] like Leon Battista Alberti (ca. 1404–1472) and Leonardo da Vinci (1452–1519), who made monumental contributions in multiple spheres of endeavour.[15] A renewed passion for pre-Christian philosophy, particularly that of Plato and, to a lesser extent, Aristotle, led to a resurgence in humanistic thought. All in all, man was beginning to timidly question his cosmic subservience and reevaluate his lowly position in the universe.

In 1341, on account of the enormous success of his epic poem, "Africa," Francesco Petrarca (1304–1374) is crowned poet laureate in Rome. His acceptance speech, which he delivers at the coronation ceremony in front of a large group of dignitaries, has gone down in his-

---

[12] Burckhardt, Jakob. *The Civilisation of the Renaissance in Italy*, Part II: The Development of the Individual, Personality "In the character of [the Italian city] states…lies…the chief reason for the early development of the Italian. To this it is due that he was the first-born among the sons of modern Europe."

[13] Ibid.

[14] 'Universal men', Ibid.

[15] Alberti was composer, painter, modeler, writer of novels, elegies and art treatises, student of physics, mathematics, canonical and civil law. Da Vinci was inventor, drawer, painter, sculptor, musician, mathematician, scientist, anatomist, geologist, astronomer, historian and cartographer.

tory as the first, true Renaissance Manifesto. Petrarch's "Coronation Oration" is about a brash a statement of humanistic fervour as you can expect from a man of the mid-fourteenth century. He begins his oration with a series of tributes to Roman writers, setting himself in immediate opposition to the medieval skepticism for pagan thought. The work of the poet, he argues, is as Cicero describes it in his oration for Aulus Licinius Archias: inspired by a "divine inbreathing." It is poet's task to follow Virgil's "sweet longing"[16] and "ascend to the peak of Mt. Parnassus," where he can flirt with the Muses. Though the climb is long and arduous, the fruits of the ascent make it well worth the toil; what the poet stands to gain is nothing less than immortal glory.

And here comes the crux of Petrarch's Oration. Far from sinful and selfish, as it may have been deemed by Augustine, the search for glory is perfectly natural: "The desire for glory is innate, not merely in the generality of men, but in greatest measure in those of some wisdom and excellence."[17]

This is the most important idea in the oration and perhaps the most influential of the entire fourteenth century. Man need not apologise for his drive to excellence. It is, in fact, perfectly natural to want it. To the self-flagellating medieval, hell-bent on putting god first and herself last, this would have appeared unconscionably hubristic.

For Petrarch, the road to personal fulfillment led, not to Empyrean, as it had for Dante a mere generation earlier, but to Parnassus; not to god, but to the *gods*. The work of the poet was divinely inspired, yes, but here the term "divine" is used metaphorically, without the heavy baggage of Christian dogma. If the artist got lucky and caught a whiff of Cicero's "divine inbreathing," he would be filled, not with the light of the *Logos*, but with something rather more elusive: a surge of inspiration more human than godly, coming from somewhere out there in the "ether" rather than from the heavens.

Over 150 years later in 1496, Pico della Mirandola would produce his own humanistic oration, his very own Renaissance manifesto: *The Oration of the Dignity of Man*. Here, he makes a point

---

[16] P. 1242
[17] P. 1245

entirely revolutionary in its application. Unlike all other things in god's cosmic vivarium, man's essence is not fixed, but moveable:

> [God] therefore took man, this creature of indeterminate image, set him in the middle of the world,[18] and said to him: "We have given you, Adam, no fixed seat or form of your own, no talent peculiar to you alone... We have made you neither of heaven nor of earth, neither mortal nor immortal, so that you may, as the free and extraordinary shaper of yourself, fashion yourself in whatever form you prefer."[19]

Man is thus unique among things and animals. He is neither of this world nor completely of the next and so is able to mould himself to determine his own essence. A fish will never escape its fishiness and an angel will never do worse than occupy his heavenly place at god's right-hand side. But man is endowed with an entirely unique capacity for upward and downward mobility.[20] If he shuts down his higher faculties (his rationality, his intellect, his ingenuity) and acts as if he doesn't possess them, he vegetates and is no better than the fish. But if, on the other hand, he exercises them carefully, if he philosophises, and accumulates knowledge, he joins the ranks of angels.

The implications were clear: man was not as far, after all, from the divine *Logos* as for centuries he'd convinced himself to be. Rather, if he delved deeply enough, he would see that he carried its spark inside him and could wield it to achieve great things.

---

[18] *Oration on the Dignity of Man*, paragraph 18, 22

[19] Ibid., paragraph 23: "It will be in your power to degenerate into the lower forms of life, which are brutish. Alternatively, you shall have the power, in accordance with the judgment of your soul, to be reborn into the higher orders, those that are divine."

[20] Ibid., paragraph 29: "If he cultivates his vegetative seeds, he will become a plant. If he cultivates his sensitive seeds, he will become a brute animal. If he cultivates his rational seeds, he will become a heavenly being. If he cultivates his intellectual seeds, he will be an angel and a son of God."

And achieve he did. The titanic advancements this new conception of man enabled are well-known enough—both in the scientific and philosophical spheres. In 1543, astronomer Nicolaus Copernicus proposed his heretical heliocentric model of the universe in his *De revolutionibus orbium coelestium*.[21] In 1609, Galileo began to use the prototypical telescope to observe the heavens, and concluded, based on said observations, that Copernicus had been right. In his *Discourse on the Method* (1637), René Descartes proposed a methodology for determining Truth by subjecting even the most sacrosanct and longest-held beliefs to a rigorous four-step test, rejecting them mercilessly if they didn't pass.[22] Taking Descartes's lead, Isaac Newton published, some fifty years later, his revolutionary *Philosophae Naturalis Principia Mathematica*[23] (1687), in which he formulated his laws of motion and universal gravitation.

The birth of experimental science was upon us. Suddenly, the universe was no longer god's impenetrable mystery; its essence no longer remote and unfathomable. By demonstrating that the Earth orbited around the sun and not vice versa, Copernicus and Galileo had called into question the divine cosmic structure set forth in the Book of Genesis and inadvertently evicted god from the heavens. By basing their factual conclusions, not on conventional wisdom or scriptural tradition, but on direct sensory observation and analytical rationalizations, Galileo and Newton had proven that man had all the tools he required—within himself—to give method to cosmic madness; to understand the world god had created and scrutinise the mechanisms underlying its basic operations. The elements around him, which had previously held merciless control of him, could now potentially be tamed and wielded to his favour.

This sea change was all-encompassing. If in our medieval infancy we had been like quivering children living under the roof of a severe and domineering father, we had now reached our rebellious adolescence and were ready to level our first challenges against paternal author-

---

[21] *On the Revolutions of the Heavenly Spheres*

[22] Part II: "Instead of a great number of precepts of which logic is composed, I believe that the four following would prove perfectly sufficient for me…"

[23] '*Mathematical Principles of Natural Philosophy*'

ity. Though not yet self-sufficient enough to leave his father's home, man was all the same slowly mustering confidence enough in his own self-worth to question his complete dependence on him. Where the humanistic revolution of the 1400s had placed man at the centre of god's cosmos, the scientific revolution of the following century provided him with a window through which to observe and systematize it. Heaven and earth were no longer distinct and separate, but connected realms; and the fibre binding them was none other than man himself.

David (Michelangelo, 1504)

In the Arts, the newfound self-assuredness of the Renaissance yielded aesthetic developments directly equivalent to their counterparts in the philosophical and scientific spheres. In 1327, Petrarch set to work on a lifelong project that was to prove to be his *magnum opus:* his *Canzoniere,* a large anthology of short poems dedicated to his beloved, Laura. Given certain surface similarities, one might be tempted, at first, to see the *Canzoniere* as Petrarch's answer to Dante's *Comedy.* Both are, after all, the crowning achievements of their respective authors, as well as their defining testaments to the power of love. And then there's the chronological proximity: less than a generation separates their conception. But between them there is a yawning aesthetic chasm. Where Dante's love for Beatrice is Augustinian in every sense, belonging more to the City of

God than of Man, Petrarch's passion for Laura is messy, turbulent, and all-over-the-shop. In one sonnet, he falls on his knees before her. In the next, he maledicts her very existence. Where Beatrice is remote, cold, and godly; Laura is very much flesh-and-blood. Dante's voyage through heaven and hell is a pilgrimage toward salvation. Petrarch's, on the other hand, is a poet's odyssey. He climbs, not toward redemption, but toward literary immortality.

In painting, a similarly humanistic sea change was taking place. In 1504, Michelangelo went to painstaking lengths to capture every anatomical nuance of the male form his *David*, proving that man himself could also be an object of artistic glorification. Where for Cimabue, two centuries earlier, style had been a frivolous human indulgence, an unnecessary distraction from Art's sole purpose (the glorification of god); for Michelangelo, it went hand in hand with subject matter and was just as critical to his aesthetic end. Man, now aware of the divine spark within him, could legitimately permit himself to put his own stamp on his creative endeavours. The technical advancements that had enabled the depiction of such anatomical precision in, not only in the *David*, but also the *Pietà* (1499) and the Sistine Chapel frescoes (1512), are themselves an indication of man's confidence in his skills and wouldn't have come about without it.

In music, a similar evolution can be traced. The 1562, *Missa Papae Marcelli*[24] by Roman composer Pierluigi Palestrina presents a clear qualitative leap from the works of his medieval predecessors. No longer fixed around a *Logos*-like drone, the harmonic structure is nuanced, fluid and mobile—like human nature itself. The harmonic Third, an interval long considered dissonant but in actual fact ubiquitous in the natural ordering of sound, is here embraced for its sumptuous, almost hedonistic sonority. A method of organizing tonality around the Circle of Fifths—another naturally occurring overtone—was beginning to slowly take shape.

In Art as in Science, therefore, man was wielding nature and systematizing it. By the time Claudio Monteverdi had penned his

---

[24] Mass for Pope Marcellus II

Orfeo (1607),[25] man had consolidated his proudest musical achievement to date—the diatonic system—and was now employing it, not merely to exult the divine, but also to add richness and nuance to the human world; in theatrical representations of human triumphs and foibles alongside masses and other sacred works.

The idea of Beauty itself had shifted, but it was no less readily available to the artist's intuition during the Renaissance than it had been in the Middle Ages. Beauty, for the thirteenth-century creative, had been the absolute moral order of the divine *Logos*, as mirrored in a clean and unmannered style. For Michelangelo and Palestrina, on the other hand, it was divine morality as perceived through the lens of man's dignified mind and represented by means of a set of man-made technical systematisations.

Villa Rotonda (Andrea Palladio, 1571)

The *Villa Rotonda* (1571) by architect Andrea Palladio derives its sense of Beauty from precisely this human imposition on divine order. In its masculine structure, symmetrical proportions, and quadrilateral form, it reflects the absolute, eternal, and unified Truth of god's moral world. But its ornamental flourishes, which are direct tributes to pre-Christian architectural forms, add subtle but unmistakable humanistic touches. Ionic capitals crown robust columns and statues of pagan deities cap each of the villa's four pediments. Atop

---

[25] Generally considered the world's oldest continuously performed opera

divine structural foundations lie humanistic embellishments, the latter complementing the former. Man finishes off what god started, and it is as if the concept of Beauty itself is no longer complete without man's intervention. Man keeps watch over all creation and one has the sudden, unshakable impression that without him, without his direct observations, none of it would have any sense at all.

And this is perhaps Renaissance Humanism's greatest contribution to metaphysics; it made man god's moral and aesthetic gatekeeper. This is echoed in Mirandola's oration:

> God the supreme Father and Architect had already fashioned this worldly home we behold… But when the work was finished, the Craftsman still longed for there to be someone to ponder the meaning of such a magnificent achievement, to love its beauty and to marvel at its vastness. So, when everything was done… He finally thought to bring forth man.[26]

In other words, god didn't *need* man, as such. The universe was, before man's creation, complete as it was. He invented man, not out of need, but desire; a desire that ran much deeper than physical necessity and bordered on the spiritual. God desired man as his divine reflection on earth. Man was no longer an incidental cosmic afterthought as he had been in the Middle Ages, but essential to the divine order of things; perhaps even the universe's very *raison d'être*. God had created moral Truth and Beauty, and he had created them for man, his magnum opus.

The Enlightenment

Captivated by the achievements of early modern science and the apparently endless reach of human understanding, philosophers

---

[26] Pg. 10, 12, 13

became preoccupied, more fervently than ever, with the comprehensive study of the mechanisms underlying human knowledge. Humanists had posited the existence of a divine spark within us. By employing it to observe the world around them, men of science had confirmed it. But the spark itself still remained a mystery. How had we come to know what we suddenly knew about the universe? By what means does knowledge enter our awareness? How can we be certain of the truth of the ideas we possess? It would be the task of the Enlightenment to address these queries; to dissect man's inner spark, understand it, and give it its proper name: "Reason."

In his *Discourse,* Descartes argued that it was upon man's *Reason* alone that he could and must build his corpus of knowledge of the truth of world around him. Reason, he argued, was an innate human faculty; universally present in and equally distributed among all members of our species.[27] Our senses are misleading and insidious. They warp our perceptions of reality in ways we don't fully understand and can, therefore, not serve as reliable indicators of truth. Reason, on the contrary, is infallible—provided, of course, it is tapped into effectively, with the precise and foolproof analytical methodology that Descartes himself lays out. So important, for Descartes, was our ability to reason that he laid it at the foundation of his philosophy. It was his first principle and his irrefutable ontological proof; we know we exist, not because we can see, feel, hear, and touch the world, but because we can think it out. Or, as he axiomatically worded it, "I think therefore I am."[28] Reason enables us to conceive, combine, and elaborate ideas about the world. And because these ideas arise independently of experience, within the consciousness itself, they are *a priori.* In other words, we have no

---

[27] Part I: "For as to the reason or sense, inasmuch as it is that alone which constitutes us men, and distinguishes us from the brutes, I am disposed to believe that it is to be found complete in each individual…"

[28] Ibid., Part IV: "I observed that, whilst I thus wished to think that all was false, it was absolutely necessary that I, who thus thought, should be somewhat; and as I observed that this truth, I think, therefore I am (COGITO ERGO SUM), was so certain…"

need of explicit recourse to our senses or direct experience to establish their truthfulness.

Partly, as a reaction to Descartes's rationalism, empiricist John Locke set forth an opposing thesis some fifty years later. In his *Essay Concerning Human Understanding* (1689), Locke argued that there could be no innate ideas. If there were, they would perforce need to be universal and all children and simpletons would possess them. And there is, patently, no such universally known idea.[29] We're therefore born tabula rasa, bereft of innate knowledge of any kind. All notions we acquire first enter our thinking minds through our senses as a direct result of our experiences. In a nod to Newton, his close personal friend, Locke picked up on the particle theory of matter and applied it to his own theory of knowledge. Throughout our lives, we register units of sensory input as simple ideas, which, when combined together, come to form more complex ideas,[30] in much the same way as particles, which constitute the smallest conceivable units of matter, combine to form larger, more complex physical structures.

The Newtonian influence may even have led Locke to elaborate his decidedly atomistic social philosophy, in which each individual in a collective is an invaluable part of the functioning whole, each being born equal by nature.[31] In his *Second Treatise of Government* (1689), Locke laid out four fundamental liberties to which, he argued, we all have right on account of the mere fact that we are born thinking,

---

[29] Book 1, Chapter 2: "There are [no innate principles] to which all mankind gives universal assent... For, first, it is evident, that all children and idiots have not the least apprehension or thought of them. And the want of that is enough to destroy that universal assent which must needs be the necessary concomitant of all innate truths: it seeming to me near a contradiction to say, that there are truths imprinted on the soul, which it perceives or understands not."

[30] Ibid., Book 2, Chapter 12: "The acts of the mind, wherein it exerts its power over its simple ideas, are chiefly...combining several simple ideas into one compound one; and thus, all complex ideas are made."

[31] *The Second Treatise of Government*, Ch. 2, Section 4: Of the State of Nature: "There being nothing more evident, than that creatures of the same species and rank, promiscuously born to all the same advantages of nature and the use of the same faculties, should also be equal one amongst another without subordination or subjection..."

reasoning beings: life, health, freedom, and property.[32] These *natural* rights are universal and inalienable; inherent in all of us irrespective of our social rank and defensible against outside violations—should the necessity of such defense arise.[33] Considering the absolutist political institutions and conditions of the time, it was a timely advance in thought. For centuries, man had lived a fearful existence under the tyranny of monarchical rule. And the unchecked power the medieval sovereign had wielded over his subjects had been rendered legitimate, at least partly, by the medieval conception of man. But if suddenly man was no longer cosmically insignificant, but a dignified moral entity in his own right, animated by the light of reason, he could be argued to possess, by virtue of his humanity alone, an integrity worthy of defense from external encroachments. Here, Mirandola's humanism acquired an added nuance. No longer was mankind, as a collective entity, worthy merely of a deference distinct from that generally shown god; now each of its single members could also lay claim to the very same by virtue of his uniqueness and separateness from all others.

Jean-Jacques Rousseau would later render explicit this nascent individualism in his *Social Contract* (1762): "So soon as the multitude is thus united in one body, it is impossible to injure one of the members without attacking the body, still less to injure the body without the members feeling the effects."[34]

It was the end of the rule of tyranny and the dawn of the Age of Reason. The sovereign had no more right, now, to gratuitously

---

[32] Chapter 8: "The state of nature has a law of nature to govern it which obliges every one: and reason, which is that law, teaches all mankind, who will but consult it, that being all equal and independent, no one ought to harm another in his life, health, liberty, or possessions…"

[33] Ibid., Ch. 2, Section 7: "And that all men may be restrained from invading others' rights, and from doing hurt to one another, and the law of nature be observed, which willeth the peace and preservation of all mankind, the execution of the law of nature is, in that state, put into every man's hands, whereby everyone has a right to punish the transgressors of that law to such a degree, as may hinder its violation."

[34] Chapter 7: The Sovereign

undermine the dignity of the individual than god did the dignity of man—not by force, fearmongering, or by any other means.

This idea would gather such momentous force throughout the century as to culminate in, arguably, the most significant political event in the West's second millennium: the French Revolution of 1789.

Man, it seemed, was finally emancipated: from superstition, from outdated traditions, and dogmas, and—finally—from his own tyrannical self. Reason had delivered him from bondage and his newfound freedom had given him legislative self-sufficiency. Beginning with the humanistic shift of the Renaissance, man had slowly usurped god as his own self-referential cosmic principle, his very own *Logos*. By the Enlightenment, the light of man's Reason had acquired a divine status of its own. Suddenly, the reasoning individual, not god, was the seat of all ethical certainty, the center of the moral universe. And here, a century or so before god was declared officially dead, we see philosophy beginning to gradually phase him out of its moral conception of the world. Through the seventeenth and eighteenth centuries, in fact, prominent thinkers—many of whom, in order to reconcile thought with faith, would at the same time desperately attempt to rework god into a system that needed him less and less—found alternative fonts to divine revelation for their moral superstructure. Descartes found it in our innate rational faculties; Locke, in our empirical observations of the world; Thomas Hobbes and Rousseau, in the social contract; Kant, in our "common human reason."[35] As the Enlightenment rolled on, god's divine light grew dimmer and the light of man's reason, brighter. It was the beginning of a self-referential, human-derived, and human-validated moral order.

In Art, man would become equally bent on legislative autonomy. The light of Reason, here wielded as a guide for the creative mind, would enable him to acquire a self-animating artistic logic that seemed to rely very little (if at all) on god's truth for its force and meaning. In music, the newly developed diatonic system was taken

---

[35] See the First Section of *Groundwork for the Metaphysics of Morals* (1785).

to new heights of dazzling complexity. In 1722 and 1742, Johann Sebastian Bach published the two books of his *Well-Tempered Clavier*: a set of twenty-four intricately contrapuntal preludes and fugues for keyboard in all major and minor keys. Midcentury, the serpentine, polyphonic idiom favoured in the high baroque would briefly give way to the restrained elegance of the *style Galant*, in which composers applied homophonic textures and balanced phrases to mirror the perfect order of the enlightened mind. These two divergent musical strands—ornamentation and purity, excess and poise—would then find their perfect synthesis in that late eighteenth century titan, Wolfgang Amadeus Mozart. In his "Jupiter Symphony" (1788), Mozart used melodic phrases of unassuming simplicity as his starting point for virtuosic thematic elaborations in his development sections.

In literature, a new form—the novel—would be employed to reinforce the liberal social ideals of Enlightenment philosophy. Two of the century's most influential authors, Samuel Richardson and Rousseau, denounced class- and gender-based infringements on individual virtue in similarly titled epistolary works: Richardson, in his *Clarissa or the History of a Young Lady* (1740); Rousseau, in his *Julie, ou la nouvelle Héloise* (1761). Beaumarchais's comedy, *The Marriage of Figaro* (1786) brought similarly political themes to the stage. In painting, the neoclassicist Jacques-Louis David created epic canvases like *The Oath of the Horatii* (1784), which depict an enlightened commitment to civic duty by means of crisp, clear detailing, and a classically geometric composition.

Clarity of intent and form, crispness of execution, balance and restraint, logic and order: these were the primary ideals upon which the eighteenth-century artistic edifice was erected. And this was no coincidence; the human mind was seen, at the time, to be characterized by the very same attributes. Like the medieval *Logos* before it, human Reason had come to be considered, by scientist and thinker alike, as a thing of perfection worthy of awe and veneration. For two hundred years, scientists had wielded it to unravel the mysteries of the physical world, and philosophers had studied it to uncover the secrets of human understanding. Man had proven capable, for the first time in history, of making scientific sense of the world around him and throughout this momentous advancement, god had played an increasingly negligible role.

In Art, a similar process of "humanisation" was unfolding. Man was no longer reliant on divine word for his natural and moral philosophy, and now he would banish it also from his conception of the aesthetically good and pure. If for the Renaissance artist, Beauty had been part human, part divine—godly in its essence and derivation, but anthropomorphic in its concrete expression—for his enlightened successors, there was little of the divine left in it. The logical order of man's reasoning mind had acquired its own divinity, supplanting god's, and the sturdy moral superstructure it afforded, which itself was a reflection of the cosmic order it had proven able to grasp, had come to dictate the manner and form of his artistic output. Beauty, too, had emancipated itself; shaken off the heavy shackles of dogma and superstition. Henceforth, it would be defined in human terms alone; as the absolute metaphysical authority conferred on the cosmos, not by god, but by man himself. A process that had been set in motion three centuries earlier had, thus, reached its fulfillment. Man was now his own self-sufficient aesthetic principle. Beauty was manmade and man-serving, like the reason-based moral world from which it derived and which it sought to emulate.

Romanticism

As the Enlightenment drew to a close, so too did the supremacy of some of its foundational presuppositions. Reason, for the eighteenth-century thinker, whether empirically or rationalistically inclined, had served as a guiding principle approximating, in its philosophical reach, the medieval *Logos*. For the rationalists, it was the direct font of all undisputable knowledge; for the empiricists, it was that inner faculty which took external sensory input and moulded it into knowledge. So great was the weight given to it in intellectual discourse, that to the average, educated gentleperson of the late eighteenth-century, it may have justifiably seemed its reign would never end.

And yet end it did, thanks to a mild-mannered professor from Konigsberg named Immanuel Kant (1724–1804). Up to a certain juncture at least, Kant's life had been largely unremarkable—at least by the standards of a man of his age, culture, and profession. He observed a regular schedule, gave classes at the local university, and never indulged in unnecessary extravagances. It was famously said that students could set their watches to the timing of his morning walks across campus. The mundanity of his day-to-day was then interrupted (at least partly) by an event that would shape the rest of his intellectual life: his discovery of the work of Scottish philosopher, David Hume (1711–1776).

Hume, the last of the great empiricists, had two generations earlier called into question the possibility of all empirical knowledge by suggesting that true understanding of cause and effect was impossible.[36] If all we could rely on was our senses, as Locke had suggested, then how could it be convincingly argued that we could deduce the causative relationship between two events, when all we could directly observe was their constant pairing in time? Merely because event B reliably follows event A, and we have never observed an instance in which this hasn't occurred, it didn't mean for Hume that A could never conceivably lead to C, D, or even E. And if the causative "thread" between discrete events was inaccessible to the senses and therefore beyond our capacity to confirm, then on what could we possibly base our claim to know any scientific fact? Hume's skepticism tied in neatly with his broader theory that we are more "feeling" than "thinking" creatures who can do no better, in our quest to understand things, than to derive our notions of the world, not from hard knowledge, but from belief, not from Locke's and Descartes's "clear and distinct ideas," but rather from something a little muddier and more slippery: what Hume called "impressions"[37] or "forceful and lively" mental representations appealing more to the passions than the intellect.

While reading Hume, Kant was thunderstruck. Suddenly "awoken from his dogmatic slumbers," he set to work on an epistemol-

---

[36] *An Inquiry Concerning Human Understanding* (1748), Section 4: Skeptical doubts about the operating of human understanding
[37] *A Treatise on Human Nature* (1740), *Book 1: Of the understanding*

ogy of his own. Agreeing with Hume on the inherent limitations of Enlightenment thought, but at the same time refusing to surrender to his colleague's extreme skepticism, Kant devised a theory that he hoped would marry the best of rationalism and of empiricism, and set about what he called a "Second Copernican Revolution."

Kant basic premise is easy enough to follow, although gleaning it from the impossibly dense prose in his *Critique of Pure Reason* (1781) is no mean feat. Without necessarily whitewashing it, it can be simplified as follows: our ideas of the world are derived, not entirely from reason (*a priori*) or entirely from experience (*a posteriori*), but from a delicate interplay of both. In this aspect, the rationalists and the empiricists had both got it only half right. Our impressions of the world enter our consciousness through our senses, yes, but when they do so, they necessarily pass through an in-built perceptual filter that reworks them in such a way as to render them intelligible to us. Without this filter, we couldn't make heads or tails of them. Both the initial prompting of the external stimulus and its subsequent, internal re-elaboration are essential to our perceptions. The first provides the content of our understanding; the second endows that content with much-needed meaning. The one half of the equation is ever-reliant on the other or, as Kant elegantly puts it: "Concepts without percepts are void; percepts without concepts, blind."[38]

The most startling—as well as the most original—feature of Kant's theory is the idea of the perceptual filter and the role it plays in re-elaborating our sensory input. For Kant, the impenetrable cognitive barrier that separates us from external reality means that we can never truly know what exists in the world around us. The thing-in-itself (*Ding-an-sich*) or the object as it exists in the *noumenal* world (the world outside our minds) is therefore distinct from the "thing-for-me" (*Ding-für-mich*) or the object as it is represented in the *phenomenal world* (the internal world of my mind). They may well be the same, Kant concedes, but since I am incapable of skipping over the perceptual barrier dividing me from the *Ding-an-sich*, I will never be able to

---

[38] *Critique of Pure Reason, Section I: Of logic in general*

know for sure.[39] For all I know, what registers to me phenomenally as a small gray mouse may, in its original, noumenal incarnation, be ten stories high, pink and yellow-striped, and have the form of a giraffe. Kant could have extended his logic by arguing that the noumenal world might not exist at all (this had been the position of George Berkeley), but thankfully, he refuses to concede this.

Now back to the perceptual filter. If I'm separated from reality by a cognitive film, the closest I can get to capturing its essence is through the lens of my own mental apparatus. But what *is* this internal apparatus? Is it reason? Sort of, but not exactly. For Kant, the human mind comes pre-configured with certain *a priori* concepts, or "universal and necessary" categories through which all our sensory perceptions pass.[40] These concepts, which include time, space, and cause-and-effect (among others) are "built-in" as part of our mental hardware.[41] This chiefly means two things. First, we are incapable of seeing the world in any other way than through the perceptual framework they provide (so a timeless or spaceless universe or one without cause-and-effect are inconceivable to us). Second, since our mind "adapts" the world in order to understand it, it can be said to be an active agent.

And herein lies Kant's Copernican Revolution. We, each and every one of us, are, in effect, sculptors of our own universe. The mind takes an external input and, rather than serving as its passive recipient, actively remodels and reworks it, rendering it coherent and endowing it with meaning. The Enlightenment had assumed a fixed reality that was rooted to its spot like a metaphysical anchor around which we, helplessly subservient to it, rotated, interpreting it to the best of our ability. Kant turned this dynamic on its head. Inverting the Copernican logic, Kant posited that it was the Earth that spun around the sun after all.

---

[39] *Ibid. Transcendental Doctrine of the Faculty of Judgment, or Analytic of Properties: General remarks on the system of principles*: "After all, the possibility of such noumena is quite incomprehensible and beyond the sphere of phenomena, all is for us a mere void."

[40] *Ibid., Transcendental Analytic*, Book 1, Chapter 1, Section 6: Of the Pure Conceptions of the Understanding, or Categories.

[41] *Ibid., Transcendental Doctrine of Elements*. First Part. *Transcendental Aesthetic*, Introduction

The mind is the centre of epistemological solar system; it is reality that changes and shifts to suit the mind's structure, not the other way around.

Kant's theory—his *Transcendental Idealism*—would serve as the starting point for a whole generation of philosophers eager to break free of the reason-worshipping and excessively objectivistic stranglehold of Enlightenment thought. Prominent German thinkers of the nineteenth century looked back on Kant with a mixture of idolatrous wonder and finicky frustration. Kant's postulations and were, at once, inspiring and unsettling to them and their life's mission became a balancing act of worshipping the master's work while simultaneously tweaking it.

For Fichte, Schelling, Hegel, and Schopenhauer, Kant had struck gold with his assertion of the mind's active role in sculpting reality. But what of reality itself? Could we really disregard the noumenal world, the *Ding-an-sich*? Would we really never again need to turn our attention to it philosophically? A world in which the world was an intellectual no-go was a no-no for the likes of these so-called German idealists, so they set about finding a comprehensive metaphysical description for its substance and inner workings.

It is an admirable feat indeed to devise a complete account of the cosmos and all things in it, but to be fair, the German idealists had a head start. Kant himself had provided all the groundwork; he had simply done so without realizing it. For the idealists, the logical next step in Kant's thought system was there, begging to be taken: if the mind is able to mould reality in such a way as to render it intelligible to us, then in what other way could we possibly explain this otherwise unthinkably virtuosic feat than by conceding that mind and reality are, in fact, one and the same?

The mind can only experience what it, in fact, already contains. The structure of the cosmos is mirrored in and reflected through the inner scaffolding of the mind, and all the objects in it are lesser or greater manifestations of this all-encompassing *Logos*-like creative and organizing energy. Time, space, cause and effect must all perforce exist externally because they exist within us. And it is because of this consistency between our internal, phenomenal reality and the external, noumenal reality that we can know what is outside us, the *Ding-an-sich*. External objects are knowable precisely because they are extensions of our own minds. The noumenal world is within our mind's grasp because it *is* our mind, made of one and the same stuff.

The German idealists all gave their unique spins on this monistic "all-is-mind" metaphysic. For Johann Fichte (1762–1814), the mind is the cosmic "self" which constitutes the totality of the real and "engenders and encompasses all being."[42] For Friederich Schelling (1775–1854) and Arthur Schopenhauer (1788–1860), it is the 'Will," an omnipresent primal being (*Ur-sein*) "to which all predicates of being apply."[43] Georg F. W. Hegel (1770–1831), who names it "Spirit," teases the concept out most completely and satisfyingly, accounting not only for the substance of all being, but its movement toward ever greater heights of self-consciousness, or what he referred to as the "absolute knowing."[44]

They may differ in the details, but these variations on a theme share the same foundation: reality is but a projection of the human mind and, therefore, possesses all its properties. Like the mind, reality is a churning, dynamic, creative, driving entity. It moves, feels, and breathes. It desires and suffers. It battles against itself and emerges from its struggles fortified. It strives toward its teleology with single-minded commitment and can rest only once its destiny is fulfilled.

The artists of the Romantic generation would take Hume's emphasis on the passions, Kant's transcendentalism, and the idealist conception of mind and lay it at the foundation of a brash new aesthetic. If man contained the entire cosmos inside himself, he could tap into this life force simply by turning inward and recognising it within. This was especially true of the artist, whose metaphysical line to the Hegelian "Absolute" was more direct than most. The artist, by virtue of her unique capacity to access "Spirit," to tap into the very fabric of reality, was uniquely poised

---

[42] *The Science of Knowledge* (1794), p. 226

[43] Schelling: *Philosophical Investigations into the Essence of Human Freedom* (1809)

[44] *The Phenomenology of Spirit* (1807), *Ch. VI: Spirit:* "The last of spirit's embodiments—spirit that endows its complete and true content with the form of self, and thereby realizes its conceptual nature even while continuing to abide within that conceptual nature—is absolute knowing."

to immerse herself in it. The artist was no longer, as she had been in the Middle Ages, a humble servant of the divine nor an objectively minded, reasoning being in the Enlightened sense, who observed reality while remaining detached from it. She was now at one with the world around her, able to draw on it, to wield it to achieve her creative ends. No longer a slave to reality nor its passive observer, the artist was now its bold and brazen conqueror. The artist/hero was born.

In 1804, Ludwig van Beethoven, who up to this point had himself been a classicist in the Mozartian vein, penned his ground-breaking *Sinfonia Eroica*.[45] Unapologetically heady and tempestuous, the *Eroica* introduced, by means of strident syncopations, slippery modulations and unrelenting dissonances, an entirely new ideal into symphonic composition: the supremacy of the artist/hero. Before the *Eroica*, composers had, to a large extent, worked collectively—as had, for that matter, artists in all other media. Style was considered shared patrimony; deriving, in other words, not from the efforts of the lone creator who, eager to gain artistic autonomy, shut himself off from his peers and worked in isolation, but rather from subtle, super-individual processes of creative cross-pollination that unfolded slowly and organically over time and could be traced to no one artist in particular. The aesthetic of Mozart had been inherited from previous generations of composers, who had worked collaboratively to prepare it. It was Mozart's task, not to create anew, but to bring to heights of ever greater perfection that which was already inherently there.

Beethoven changed this. By putting his own stamp on his music and willfully steering it away from the work of his predecessors, he made a clear and bold statement, game-changing in its effects: it was the individual, not the collective, who was the ultimate font of artistic inspiration. His *Eroica* had, not by coincidence, originally been dedicated to Napoleon, the heroic figure *par excellence*. And although Beethoven would, upon learning that his dedicatee had arrogantly crowned himself emperor, later scratch out the leader's name from the original manuscript, the principle remained: this was the hero's symphony, a homage to the glory of individual brilliance and achievement.

---

[45] *Heroic Symphony*

Wanderer Above the Sea of Fog (Caspar David Friederich, 1818)

Here, "hero" had a twofold meaning: the philosopher-king who would save the world and the artist-genius who would save people's souls. And the notion of saving souls was not incidental. The Romantic artist had gradually come to see himself as the modern embodiment of an ancient archetype: the high priest or wizard, more pagan than Christian in spirit and function; a special being, gifted with rare, supernatural powers, who had more immediate access to high ideals than the common man. The artist/hero served as a conduit to an otherworldly plane, the Hegelian "Absolute," and all those seeking contact with it would need to first pass through him. This explains why, in his *Wanderer Above the Sea of Fog* (1818), painter Caspar David Friedrich depicted his hero amid nature, casting his gaze over a rugged, emotionally charged landscape: only the natural world seemed to offer the nineteenth-century painter the transcendence he lusted after.

As the century rolled on and the artist's ego grew, so too did the creative license he would concede himself. No longer satisfied with having reinvented musical aesthetics, Beethoven would, with his later symphonies, reinvent himself afresh with every new work, producing a tour de force of motivic terseness in his Fifth, a bucolic reverie in his Sixth (1808), and—his final will and testament—the mighty Ninth (1824) which, exceeding by far the average length of the genre and introducing choir and vocal soloists, seemed to set future generations of composers a standard of excellence impossible to match.

But match him they did. A mere few years after Beethoven's death, Frenchman Hector Berlioz wrote his *"Symphonie Fantastique,"*[46] a rambunctious masterpiece, equal parts symphony and programmatic reverie. Subtitled *"Episode de la vie d'un artiste,"*[47] the symphony narrates the hellish descent into madness of a sensitive young artist tormented by his obsessive love for an unattainable woman—his *"idée fixe."*[48] When the *Symphonie* was premiered in 1830, it proved every bit as startling and fresh as the work of his German forebear. Harmonically and structurally, it was worlds away from the poise and restraint of eighteenth-century rationalism. Aesthetically, it rendered explicit what had merely been alluded to in Beethoven: that the artist was a tragic hero, burdened to feel life more intensely than the average person but, simultaneously, able to savour it more deeply; that the artist could access the highest levels of excellence only if she was true to her feelings and permitted herself to express them unapologetically. Berlioz was, in this respect, Beethoven's direct heir, music's second grand revolutionary hero, and for this reason his place in the musical firmament is secure. For, without the groundwork he laid, the harmonic upheaval Wagner would later effect with his Music Drama *Tristan und Isolde* (1865) would have been all but impossible.

Romanticism was the West's first great age of artistic experimentation, directly predating and preempting twentieth-century modernism. The insatiable thirst for creative novelty—which we now take for granted but, until the nineteenth century, had been anomalous—was born of the Romantic sense of individual supremacy. After Beethoven, it would no longer be acceptable for any serious artist to speak the same stylistic language as his influences. "Originality," or the idea that in order to be artistically relevant one had to create one's own aesthetic, quickly diffused itself and became the norm. All artists working subsequently, including those in the present day, have operated within this paradigm. And as we shall see, individualistic aesthetics and the drive to originality would have far-reaching, if unintended consequences,

---

[46] "Fantastical Symphony"
[47] "Episodes from the life of an artist"
[48] Fixed idea

sowing the seeds of the nihilism and relativism that would characterize much artistic production in the following epoch.

Modernism

Nietzsche's parable is well-known enough. A madman lights a lantern in the early hours and runs into a marketplace, shouting, "I seek God!" Reacting with indignation to the laughter of the towns-people, he jumps in their midst and cries, "Where is God? I will tell you… God is dead. And we have killed him… How shall we comfort ourselves, murderers of all murderers?"[49]

It was the year 1891. Friedrich Nietzsche published the final installment of his philosophical novel, *Thus Spoke Zarathustra*, naming therein a specter which, having emerged fifty years earlier in Russia, had begun to cast its shadow over Western Europe: the specter of nihilism. At first glance, the above-quoted parable may appear hyperbolic. But when Nietzsche spoke of deicide, he was not posturing for dramatic effect. The 'de-theification' of all human thought which, as we have seen, was first set in motion in Renaissance Italy, had by the end of the nineteenth century reached a point of such all-encompassing influence as to be virtually undeniable by any serious thinker as the new intellec-tual paradigm. "God is dead," to Nietzsche meant "god is irrelevant" (which, needless to say, wouldn't have had the same ring to it). Given the philosopher's strong atheistic bent, it doubtless also meant "god never existed at all." And this declaration of godlessness, brazen though it may sound, should come as no surprise; the centuries-long progres-sion just mentioned had more than paved the way for it.

The nonexistence of god was not a new idea; medieval theologians like Thomas Aquinas had gone to great lengths to rebut it.[50] Before the nineteenth century, however, atheism was a mere thought experiment; a hypothetical nonreality utilised by religious thinkers as a tool to consol-

---

[49] *Thus Spoke Zarathustra,* Part II (1891)
[50] Aquinas proposed, in his *Summa Theologica*, five proofs for the existence of God (First Part, Treatise on the One God, The Existence of God)

idate their theistic convictions. But hypothesis had now morphed into a very vivid and, in certain respects, nightmarish reality. Suddenly, without an all-powerful and all-loving being at its helm, the universe was cold and empty with nothing but dead, mechanistic forces animating its movements and determining its fate. Man was left alone in the dark with no benevolent father looking down on him, no infinitely just judge ensuring a blissful eternal life as reward for a pious earthly one.

And now for Nietzsche's *coup de grace*. In this godless world order, he argued, not only would you have to renounce happiness in the afterlife; you would most probably have to resign yourself to misery and chaos in this one as well. For if god didn't exist, there was no one to help us tell right from wrong, no one to inform us how to live justly. Worse still, with no morally infallible being to decree it from on high, there could be no right or wrong in the first place, no good or evil—only relative judgments thereof, which, because they were man-derived, could by necessity be nothing but arbitrary. This is the nihilistic argument in a nutshell. If god alone can determine Truth, universal and eternal, then in a godless universe, there can exist no such Truth. And in a world with no Truth, there can be no immutable values; no single way of living that, by universal consensus, can be judged just and good across all times and cultures. If this was true, Nietzsche asked, how then were we to live? If there was no Truth, no infallible font of right and wrong, from where were we to derive a coherent morality? Or a sense of purpose and meaning? What would prevent social order from degenerating into chaos?

This ethical quandary had been preempted by, arguably, the century's greatest moralist and an idol of Nietzsche's: Fyodor Dostoevsky. In Dostoevsky's *Brothers Karamazov* (1880), Ivan, the most coldly intellectual figure in the novel, is debating with his deeply religious brother Alexey, when he orgiastically affirms: "If God doesn't exist, all is permitted!"[51] Here, Dostoevsky was articulating a bone-chilling fear that had plagued him his entire creative life. Having noted the moral nihilism that had first emerged in the 1840s with anarchist thinker Mikhail Bakunin, Dostoevsky, a devout Orthodox Christian,

---

[51] P. 294

decided to combat it head-on and wield his literary gift to help divert the terrifying lawlessness he felt was sure to bring about. In his last fifteen years, in fact, he produced most of his greatest masterpieces: *Crime and Punishment* (1866), *The Possessed* (1872), *The Dream of a Ridiculous Man* (1877), and *The Brothers Karamazov.* All these are dedicated precisely to this urgent moral task.

Nietzsche and Dostoevsky's fears of a godless chaos are, for the most part, unjustified—as I will explain later. Nonetheless, it is important to keep in mind that, to newly atheistic people still grieving the loss of a heavenly father, they would have felt very real. Let us furthermore not underestimate their tenacity. The ethical stresses arising from a godless universe have persisted to the present and the history of philosophy of the next 130 years can, with little exaggeration, be seen as a drawn-out attempt to satisfactorily allay them.

The earliest of these attempts was, I dare say, an immature one: if god doesn't exist, then man is god. In the absence of a divine commander, man can do whatever he wants and become whoever he wants. He could devise his own morality and, if whim gets the better of him, discard and refashion it.

Dostoevsky and Nietzsche both explicitly proposed this solution, in differing contexts: Dostoevsky, in *The Brothers Karamazov*: "Once humanity has rejected God...the man-God will be born"; Nietzsche, in *Zarathustra* with his notorious *Übermensch*[52] theory: "Man is something that shall be overcome...(The *Übermensch*) is the lightning; he is the frenzy."[53]

Writing some sixty years later, the existentialist Jean-Paul Sartre provided his own spin. "Existence precedes essence,[54]" he wrote in *Existentialism is a Humanism* (1946)—roughly meaning this: because there is no "one" cosmic Truth, we all come into this world void of eternal, immutable qualities. We're born, in other words, simply exist-

---

[52] At times translated as "Overman" and at others, "Superman," the *Übermensch*, for Nietzsche, was an individual who had succeeded in overcoming his enslavement to life-negating social conventions, and lived by his own, independently devised moral system.

[53] Part 1

[54] Part 1: *The Humanism of Existentialism*

ing—*tabula rasa*, one might almost say. The various bits and pieces that come to constitute our essence, we acquire slowly over time and mostly in haphazard fashion. Ultimately, this meant one thing for Sartre: we are free[55]—completely and utterly. If the qualities we possess are all acquired and not innate, it means we can deselect them at will and replace them with others of our choosing. We are, in other words, man-gods, able to make of ourselves what our fancy desires and limited in this respect by our ambition and imagination alone.

As leftfield a proposition this may seem, it is far from a historical anomaly. The death of a metaphysical god was, after all, declared just as the godliness of the individual was in the ascendancy. The Romantics had not yet anointed themselves as divine but, convinced as they were of their priestliness, of their mystical (and very godlike) powers, they had been but a small step away. With the advent of nihilism, they were able to take the final plunge. The individual was, no longer sage and sorcerer, but supreme deity; no longer shaper, but creator of destinies; no longer a conduit of the transcendent, but its lord and master. Like Napoleon a century earlier, modern man had removed god's crown and placed it on his own head. Individualism and nihilism had fused to form an existentialist's solution to godlessness.

Modernists working at the turn of the century—in musical, literary, and visual forms alike—quickly applied this solution to their art, proving eager to make the most of what, for Dostoevsky, had been an unambiguously dire situation. If there was no god, so be it—the true artist never needed him anyway. Just as he'd killed god and overturned all Truth and Meaning he'd once bestowed, the man-god would now turn his attention to art and bring to bear on it the full force of his newfound omnipotence. It was a new world, and for the first time in history, man was free. Having long feuded with his celestial father, long rebelled against his authoritarian ways, he'd finally cut all ties and left his paternal home. He was dazed and confused, yes, but independent; no longer accountable morally to anyone but himself. Across all major

---

[55] Ibid.: "That is the idea I shall try to convey when I say that man is condemned to be free. Condemned, because he did not create himself, yet, in other respects is free; because, once thrown into the world, he is responsible for everything he does."

Art forms, this brand of Nietzschean *Übermenschheit* found direct and unequivocal expression. For if there were no universal values in life, how could there be any in Art? If in life, the freedom afforded by the existential void was total, what could stop this absolute freedom from extending also to painting, music, and literature?

In 1908, composer Arnold Schönberg premièred his atonal "Second String Quartet" to a dumbfounded Viennese public. Eight years later, maverick painter Pablo Picasso presented his *Demoiselles d'Avignon* in that other European capital of culture, Paris. The two works, perfectly parallel in social significance and impact, shocked the bourgeois and helped kick-start the modernist revolution.[56]

Picasso's five *demoiselles* are angular and otherworldly. Their faces range from benignly deformed to outright demonic. On and around them, perspective is twisted in typical cubist fashion; their limbs are unnaturally contorted and their bodies, eerily out of proportion. They seem to stand against a vortex in which time and space are refracted and in contemplating it, we may be forgiven for thinking our senses are being duped.

Les demoiselles d'Avignon
(Pablo, Picasso)

---

[56] For the impact of Picasso's Demoiselles, see Hilton Kramer essay, reflections on Matisse's, in The Triumph of Modernism: The Art World 1985–2005: "With the bizarre painting that appalled and electrified the cognoscenti, which understood that Les Desmoiselles was at once a response to Matisse's Le Bonheur de vivre (1905–1906) and an assault upon the tradition from which it derived, Picasso effectively appropriated the role of avant-garde "wild beast"—a role that, as far as public opinion was concerned, he was never to relinquish."

Schönberg's work is similarly mind-bending. The *Quartet* starts innocuously enough, in a form of diatonicism pushed to its outer limits, noticeably more jarring than the Strauss of the *Sinfonia Domestica*,[57] but nonetheless palatable for the contemporary audience. Twenty-three minutes in, however, the music takes a dark and unexpected turn. A soprano intones the sombre verses of poet Stefan George: *"Tief ist die trauer die mich umdüstert."*[58] The music loses its tonal bearings and embraces a hitherto unheard chromatic dissonance. The result is a thoroughgoing atonality that affords the ear no anchor to latch onto and proves most apt at conveying the moral ambivalence of the time.

In both *Les Demoiselles* and the Second Quartet, the man-god is clearly at work. Empowered by the freedom granted by the nihilistic Zeitgeist, Picasso and Schönberg had become charged, at the dawn of the new century, with an irrepressible iconoclastic fervour. They had come to look upon the ancient conventions of their respective forms with skepticism; as no longer sacred and infallible, but fluid and imminently subjectable to change. Visual realism and diatonicism, which since the dawn of modern Art in the Renaissance had been sturdy pillars of Western painting and music, were made the object of a comprehensive reevaluation. The modernist revolution had not come from nothing, to be sure. In music, the meandering and ambiguous harmonies of Wagner's *Tristan* and, in painting, the shimmering impressionism of Claude Monet's *Sunrise* (1874) had paved the way for it. But it was Picasso and Schönberg who would dive headfirst into the abyss, consigning, by means of a few thousand brush strokes and quavers, centuries of achievement in Western Art to the proverbial dustbin.

The example they set was followed avidly by all their successors—with no exception. Alban Berg and Anton Webern, disciples of Schönberg, studiously advanced the atonality of their mentor; Berg, by mixing it in with a late Romantic grandiloquence in his opera, *Wozzeck* (1925); Webern, by stripping it down to its bare bones in pointillist works like his *Symphony* (1926). In a parallel musical nar-

---

[57] German composer Richard Strauss wrote his *Sinfonia Domestica* (Domestic Symphony) in 1904, four years before Schönberg's Second Quartet

[58] "Deep is the sadness that sweeps over me."

rative, a thirty-one-year-old Igor Stravinsky premièred, in 1913, his fiercely asymmetrical ballet *Rite of Spring*, doing for rhythm what Schönberg had done for tonality five years earlier. Georges Braque— who, alongside Picasso, is credited with having cofounded Cubism— completed, in an astonishing six-year burst of creativity, such notable works as *Maisons à l'Éstaque* (1908), *Violon et palette* (1909), *Portrait of a Woman* (1910), *Nature morte* (1913), and *Man with a Guitar* (1914)—all of which rival, if not surpass the work of his more famous colleague for their uncompromising radicalism.

Literary modernism was a little slower to get going, but once it did, there was no stopping it. In 1913, the year of Stravinsky's *Rite*, Marcel Proust found a publisher for the first of the seven volumes of his colossus, *À la recherche du temps perdu*.[59] Nine years later, James Joyce published the first installment of his own answer to the *Recherche*: the sprawling, vexing *Ulysses*. The two works present unmissable parallels. Both are of formidable length (at 1.3 million words, Proust's *Recherche* is generally agreed to be the longest novel ever written). Both see the world through the eyes of highly sensitive, neurotic types who are on the hunt for meaning in a world reluctant to provide it. And most importantly, both paint a vivid picture of a decadent, nihilistic culture, deploying to this end aesthetic tools every bit as earth-changing as those of Picasso, Stravinsky, and Schönberg.

Proust filled the *Recherche* to bursting point with sentences so serpentine, that one has to reread the longest of them several times in order to properly register their meaning. In *Ulysses*, Joyce systematically dismantled language, twisting the meaning of words, subverting traditional syntax and constantly coining neologisms—the effect of which is a willful bamboozlement of the reader. In both, a linear plotline takes back seat to less conventional structuring principles. Flow is attributable less to story arch and character development than to an ongoing commentary on the nature of language, and to a reflection on interconnected ideas, big and small. Just as Picasso and Schönberg had done away with realism and diatonicism respectively, Proust and Joyce had now done away with traditional narrative. The literary man-god, like his counterparts in music

---

[59] *In Search of Lost Time*

and painting, was here willfully undoing history, destroying the old and rebuilding Art from its very foundations.

The experimentalism that had seen its first tentative stirrings in Romanticism had now become Art's unquestionable governing force. For the modernist, no idea or value was sacred, not even those that had remained unchallenged for centuries. Originality was now seen as the supreme intellectual and aesthetic virtue and its exponents pursued it with the fervour of martyrs. Modernism had become a sort of religious creed. It is telling, in this sense, that for the first time in history, Art saw a flourishing of so-called *manifestos*—Filippo Marinetti's 1909 *Manifesto del futurismo* being the first in a series that also included those by the Dadaists (1916), the Bauhaus architects (1919), and the Surrealists (1924). These were not unlike sets of holy commandments; prescriptive codes that regulated, in the strictest terms, the set of aesthetic practices and outcomes considered acceptable for the subscribers to a given style or school.

The first page of the 1909
Manifesto del futurismo by Filippo Marinetti

Manifestos were made necessary because the "rules" they prescribed were not intuitable. They had been more or less artificially devised and, therefore, had to be inculcated by moderately coercive means. Modernism was distinguishable from preceding movements also for this reason: it was overtly dogmatic. In previous eras, aesthetic dogmas were not absent but functionally organic and therefore, for the most part, only "softly" enforced. They evolved by a process analogous to common law judicial precedents. When an influential artist made an advancement that was perceived to be likely to contribute something legitimately good and beautiful, it was taken up by other artists and, slowly, it diffused itself as common practice. But in an era of violent and sudden rupture with the past, this approach would no longer suffice. An acceptable agenda for the future could not be left to nature to "sort out"; it had to be expressly deliberated and catalogued, much as it would be in a civil law code.

This tendency toward dogmatic absolutism would reach its zenith in the high Modernism of the post-WWII period. Now the "new" was not merely the noblest of artistic virtues, it was an absolute imperative. The old had to make way for the new, no matter what the cost. And no artist expecting to be taken seriously could exhibit even the vaguest hint of reactionism. The first wave of modernists had had the right idea, but they'd been too meek. Schönberg, Picasso and co. had left too tangible a connection to an ancient past they should have ruthlessly denounced and overthrown.

In music, it would be up to three composers in particular to rectify this botch-up: Pierre Boulez, Karlheinz Stockhausen, and John Cage. Boulez and Stockhausen, in works like *Polyphone X* and *Kreuzspiel* (1951), extended Schönberg's tonal serialism to all other musical parameters, including dynamics and durations, creating scores that were mathematically, almost maniacally predetermined. Going to the opposite extreme, Cage, father of indeterminate music, sought to minimise the role of the composer, if not eliminate it altogether. In his *4'33'* (1952), the performer is instructed to sit with his instrument in front of a blank score in complete silence, and not make a single sound from the beginning of the piece to the end. With works like his *No. 5, 1948*, painter Jackson Pollock took the abstractism championed by Kandinsky a step further, and did away with all discernible, earthly subject matter, filling his work instead with unidentifiable, amorphous spatters.

No. 5, 1948 (Jackson Pollock)

It is no small irony that, in spite of the hard-lined Modernist approach to aesthetics, there never came to be a sole orthodox code universally seen as representing the movement more faithfully than any other. Since there was no Modernist "central governing body," and also since Modernism was individualistic in essence, there emerged, instead, a curious situation in which the prevailing aesthetic climate was, at once, hyper-dogmatic and hyper-pluralistic; one in which there existed a multitude of related but differing schools, each convinced that it, more than any other, held the key to the future of Art. Heady modernists who had stayed true to Nietzsche's *Übermensch* ideal and Sartre's concept of existential freedom, filled the nihilistic void with aesthetic values that they, as godlike aesthetes, had judged themselves competent to create and prescribe. The prevailing value-lessness had afforded them this total creative freedom, given them a sense of duty to exercise it and legitimated their efforts to do so.

Part II: A Critique of Postmodern Relativism

The Death of Beauty

It is my conviction that Modernism constitutes the beginning of a third "meta era" in the history of post-pagan Western Art and Beauty. The first, which we covered only briefly, began with the rise of Christianity in the fourth century and was characterised by aesthetic absolutism; god determined Meaning and Beauty, man helplessly followed. The second, arising in the Renaissance and ending with late Romanticism, saw man and god working side by side, with the first slowly taking control of domains previously governed by the second. The third began with the death of god and the ensuing nihilistic upheaval. God was made redundant and man took his place as supreme aesthete. These were, in order, the era of god, the era of man, and the era of the man-god.

These aesthetic meta eras find their direct metaphysical equivalents, respectively, in theism, humanism, and nihilism. The first of these posits the existence of a godly Truth, immutable and eternal. The second suggests an innate human Truth (more or less) sanctioned by god. And the third categorically refutes both; there is no eternal Truth, neither divine nor human, so one would do well to stop chasing after it and, instead, live by a truth of one's own making. Theism, which by necessity yielded an absolutist conception of the universe, imposed an equally incontestable image of Beauty; Beauty was god, including all that was decreed by his divine *Logos* and lay in accordance to his divine plan. Humanism took the absolutist sense of the good and beautiful once reserved for god alone and applied it to man; Beauty is man, because man was created by god and Beauty was created by god for man. Nihilism then kicked god out of the picture altogether and, in doing so, made any absolutist aesthetic affirmations impossible. If we had always depended, in one way or another, on god for our conception of Beauty, how could Beauty be said to exist at all without him?

Modernism rigorously applied these nihilistic conclusions to Art. It did away with Beauty in much same way as it had done away with practically everything else, leaving Art stripped of the very core ingredient that had always defined it. To the late Romantic even, Art in the 1950s and '60s would have appeared unrecognizable. Never in history had there been such a seismic shift in ideology, never such a radical "transvaluation of values," never such a cold-blooded "aestheticide." Without necessarily knowing it, all major Modernist artists from Schönberg to Cage, from Picasso to Pollock, had systematically broken down Beauty. By the time the Fluxus artists rose to prominence in the '60s, Beauty as we'd known it for five hundred years was no more. "Beauty is dead," Nietzsche may well have said. "And we, murderers of murderers, have killed it."

Ironically for Nietzsche, who was a firm believer in the ennobling quality of Art, it was the *Übermensch* himself who'd turned out to be the "murderer of all murderers." The man-god had decided Beauty didn't exist and had set about instituting strict dogmas aimed at eliminating all references to it. It is a curious thing indeed that an ideology as nihilistic as this one yielded, as an immediate knee-jerk response, an uncompromising artistic dogmatism rather than the relativism it so plainly contained in itself. For if Beauty really didn't exist, then it shouldn't have mattered whether it was kept alive or not; if there were no eternal, immutable ideals, then surely all remnants of Beauty could have been allowed to coexist alongside other, equally mutable, perishable ideals and at most be renamed and reframed.

The onset of this kind of relativistic open-mindedness would have to wait until the advent of Postmodernism in the late 1960s—almost eighty years after Nietzsche's famous declaration. Here, the logic of the man-god would collapse under the weight of its egotistical absurdity. God didn't exist—this was, by now, practically incontestable. And if he didn't exist outside of man, he quite clearly couldn't exist within him either. Man's insistence to crown himself supreme aesthete in god's place had proven itself to be nothing more than hubris; a shallow attempt to replace an old, false idol with a newer, even more dubious one. For if all-powerful and all-knowing entity had proven himself unable to rule the cosmos, had "died" trying, how could man, pathetic and weak as he was, expect to succeed where he'd failed?

In his *The Postmodern Condition* (1979), philosopher Jean-Francois Lyotard defined Postmodernism as an "incredulity toward metanarratives." This, I feel, is apt. By "metanarrative," Lyotard meant underlying conceptions of the world that allow us to remain firmly and earnestly rooted in our metaphysical reality and live in a state of genuine investment in it. Common metanarratives include the infallibility of scientific inquiry, the linear progress of history, but also, as we have seen, the unquestionable existence of ideals such as Truth, Meaning, and Beauty. Without a sincere belief in such metanarratives, we become aloof and despondent. Unable to sink our metaphysical feet into the foundations of reality, we detach ourselves emotively from it and life itself becomes comical because we begin to see it as if from afar, where its underlying absurdity is exposed. With the advent of nihilism, many of the world's most cherished moral metanarratives had already been done away with. One, however, had persisted (mostly because it had replaced many of the old): the ideal of the man-god. But at the hand of the Postmodernists, this too would be disbanded, leaving little to prevent man from coming loose from his ethical moorings.

The idea of a philosophical removal from life, of an affective detachment from its absurdity was, by the way, not new. Albert Camus had proposed it in his *Myth of Sisyphus* in 1942. Here, Camus described what he termed the "'Absurd," which, in his conception, didn't mean that existence was inherently irrational per sé (such a proposition would be ridiculous, for it would suggest that the universe had created itself expressly with human logic in mind, and then intentionally eschewed it). Rather, the Absurd was a human sentiment, existing in man's mind alone. It referred to the internal ten-

sion, the consternation we experience when our need for metaphysical order clashes with the universe's obstinate refusal to furnish it.[60]
Camus's solution to the Absurd and the anguish it caused was a sober
but optimistic resilience that amounted to a daily revolt. "One must
imagine Sisyphus happy," he wrote at the end of *The Myth*, referring
to the ancient Greek hero who, as punishment for his arrogance, was
condemned by the gods to roll a boulder up a hillside for all eternity.
Life for all of us is just as meaningless as it is for Sisyphus. But rather
than kill ourselves on account of it, which is the first solution that
often comes to mind, we must roll up our sleeves, put on a big smile
and resolve to live well in spite of it.

This cheerful indifference in the face of life's absurdity would
be adopted by the Postmodernist as his modus operandi. Dramatists
Samuel Beckett and Eugène Ionesco, important Postmodernist
precursors, took Camus's conception of the Absurd and coloured
their stage plays with it. In Beckett's *Waiting for Godot* (1953) and
Ionesco's *Rhinocéros* (1959), characters are vexed by sinister metaphysical conundrum. They await answers to existential queries in an
irrational and menacing world that proves, time and again, unwilling
to provide them. Though the underlying message is a dark and tragic
one (life is privy of meaning and all attempts to find it are pointless), its method of communication is comical. In *Godot*, all common
logic is subverted, leaving the characters thwarted in their actions.
But they shrug off their misfortune and make light of it, leaving the
viewer undecided as to whether to respond with laughter or tears.

Irony and irreverence, in fact, seemed to the Postmodernist
the only just response to the Absurd. This was, in large part, a reaction against the heavy-handedness of the gargantuan modernist ego,
which had now revealed itself laughable. Modernism had gone too
far, taking its pathological obsession with the new to an aesthetic
dead end and leaving the artist with nowhere to go but in one sense
"up" and in another, "down." Having identified as risible attempts
to forcibly assert aesthetic Truth by means of hard-lined dogma, and

---

[60] Ch 1, *An Absurd Reasoning*: "This divorce between man and his life, the actor
and his setting, is properly the feeling of absurdity."

having at the same time thoroughly absorbed the full logical implications of the nonexistence of Beauty (the ultimate Art metanarrative), the Postmodernist reacted, first, by withdrawing from a world he could no longer rely on metaphysically, and then, able to gaze upon it from a great height, bursting into uncontrollable laughter over the hopeless mess of it.

The words of Kierkegaard come to mind:

> As I grew up, I opened my eyes and saw the real world and I began to laugh. And I haven't stopped since. I saw that the meaning of life was to get a livelihood; that the goal of life was to be a high-court judge; that the brightest joy of love was to marry a well-off girl; that wisdom was the majority said it was... That's what I saw. And I laughed.[61]

It's astonishing that Kierkegaard should have preempted, by 120 years, the Postmodern skepticism toward metanarrative, anticipating even Camus. Or perhaps it is rather astonishing that it should have taken humanity so long to apply it. But apply it we have—in an aesthetic in which the absurdity of Truth and the futility of earnestness is affirmed at every turn; in which Art is no longer definable and, therefore, subjectable to all manner of derisions; in which high and lowbrow recklessly intermingle and stylistic conventions are toyed with sadistically; in which the pursuit of the new constitutes little more than a battering of the old; and in which any attempt of an artist to take the ennobling aspect of his art seriously is considered hubristic and misguided.

With his collection of short stories, *Lost in the Funhouse* (1968), John Barth invented "metafiction." Highly irreverent and self-reflexive, this style of narration rested on a notion that Barth himself had outlined in a previous work[62]: literary "exhaustion." With high

---

[61] *Either/Or* (1843)
[62] *The Literature of Exhaustion* (1967)

Modernism, Barth argued, fiction had reached an endpoint having definitively exhausted all expressive and stylistic possibilities. The contemporary writer, therefore, had no choice but to take a radically different tack; to rise above the form itself, creating not works of fiction, but works that resembled fiction, spoke of fiction, dissected it, ironised it, and provided a commentary on it. Joyce had, with his language-dismantling *Ulysses,* already hinted at this method, but Barth would place it at the centre of his aesthetic. There ensued, in the following decade, a number of works from Barth's literary contemporaries that followed his example. Kurt Vonnegut's *Slaughterhouse-Five* (1969), Thomas Pynchon's *Gravity's Rainbow* (1973), Italo Calvino's *If on a Winter's Night a Traveler* (1979), and Umberto Eco's *The Name of the Rose* (1980) all present many of most recognizable Postmodern trademarks: self-reflexive commentary, unreliable narrators, intertextuality, and unwavering irony.

Music was quick to catch on. In 1969, Luciano Berio premièred his *Sinfonia*: a sprawling, grotesque work for massive symphony orchestra in which eight vocalists provide, as the piece unfolds, a running commentary of self-referential gags and musical observations. Five years later, Russian Alfred Schnittke wrote his First Symphony (1974), juxtaposing, in it, a variety of different musical idioms and thereby inventing musical polystylism. In 1976, Philip Glass did the unthinkable and returned music to its diatonic roots, re-introducing simple triadic harmonies and near-conventional harmonic progressions—but with a twist. His music was characterised by—as he termed it—"repetitive structures," or small rhythmic and motivic figures repeated *ad nauseam*. All these were attempts at creative freshness that involved a thoroughly Postmodern, "meta" perspective; an ability to see conventions and styles from a detached, ironic viewpoint.

An Attempt to Define Beauty

Enough has been said of the Postmodern spirit to convey an adequate picture of it. In our time, the artist is no longer high priest and certainly no longer god, but something of a court jester; a prestidigitator toying with a spark of creative energy that has been proven to be, not divine after all, but absurd and, for this reason, worthy not of exaltation but of derision. The artist is no longer making manifest universal Truth, as she had done uninterruptedly for centuries. Nor, as was the case through modernism, is he any longer fashioning his own individual truths he can sublimate on an altar of his own aesthetic egotism. Now, the Absurd has dethroned the divine as master of the universe, as art's overarching governing principle. What was once holy and venerable is now grotesque, the object of gest and mockery. No artist now, who takes herself seriously, can allow herself to be serious at all. Ironically enough, irony is the new earnestness.

For the first time in history, Beauty is now considered highly personal and, for this reason, can be deemed nonexistent. For, if something exists in a way that varies inevitably from person to person, it exists only in its differing forms. And that which gives an entity its form, what makes it recognizable and sets it apart from other entities, is essential unity, not diversity. Now this unity is lacking and what I call beautiful, you may deem ugly and vice versa. All Art, no matter how nonconformant it may be to traditional conceptions, can be considered Art, because Art itself has lost its universal qualities. And those who insist on imposing universality on it, on attributing divinity to it, are mocked for their snobbery, derided as outdated, pompous, or unenlightened. Dare to question the merit of an artist painting with her own vagina[63] and you're assailed by the Postmodernist for your closed-mindedness. Casually mention that Philip Glass's beloved repetitive structures may be a little too repetitive and you're snarled at for not being able to appreciate minimalism's internal logic on its own terms. It's a strange set of affairs indeed, that which we find ourselves in aesthetically; one in which the only prevailing dogmatism is a sort of anti-dogma that is defended as stridently by its puritanical standard-bearers as if it actually existed, as if it were built

---

[63] At the Perpetual Fluxus Festival in New York in 1965, artist Shigeko Kubota assumed a crouching position over a sheet of paper on the floor with a brush affixed to the crotch of her underwear and painted abstract lines in blood red paint. She named the piece *Vagina Painting*.

and founded on a set of sturdy values and principles, when it's the absence of these very principles that constitutes its reason for being.

In all this, I imagine a collective self-deception to be at work; one having to do with a peculiar facet of human psychology: *cognitive dissonance*. On an individual level, when things start to go wrong in our lives, when some critical event has befallen us that causes us to question old values we once held true, and our world begins to reveal the absurdity of its logic, we are startlingly good, at least for a period of time, at denying that any of this is going on at all, or—more precisely—denying its importance. Before the full gravity of the situation bears down on us, we march on for a period of time, justifying the death of the old order by arguing its sudden irrelevance, denying the value of what's been lost. In the process, we blind ourselves to the destruction the loss is causing. To paraphrase an idea of Nietzsche, in times of trouble we often call it virtue when our vices grow weak;[64] when we lose sight of our real virtues and are too disoriented to see our shortcomings for what they are.

Humanity functions similarly to this on a collective level, I believe, and an analogous principle is at work in the current aesthetic climate. We are going through a period of collective moral reevaluation, a sort of civilizational quarter-life crisis. And it's not so much that we have lost our innate sense of what is beautiful in Art—for we couldn't have lost this any more than we could lose our innate sense of right and wrong—but we are, admittedly, confused by it. And it's because we are confused by Beauty, its definition and purpose, that we deny its importance—in order to feel a semblance of certainty amid the chaos. If dogmatic absolutism has caused so much strife in the past, says our collective consciousness, how could it continue to serve us in the future? And if it can't serve us, it not only must be rendered inapplicable to contemporary life and art, but also claimed never to have been valid at all. Postmodernism is the contemporary aesthetic manifestation of this collective self-deception. In a world of valueless relativism, where any affirmation of universal Truth is

---

[64] "There are those who call it virtue when their vices grow lazy." *Thus Spoke Zarathustra*, Part II

risible, the idea of immutable beauty in Art is considered outdated piffle. We don't need it in order to create art, says the Postmodernist. And what's more, we never needed it to begin with, even when we thought we did because it really never existed at all. One can almost hear the words of the Kakanian Ulrich[65] when his friend Walter questions him on the meaning of life: "Meaning? I get on quite well without it."[66] Postmodernism makes it its job to ensure we all "get on quite well" without Beauty, by convincing us of the futility of affirming its unquestionable existence.

Sadly, for the Postmodernist, we can no more get on without Beauty than we can get on without the sense that our life has any meaning. We are just as dependent on the former as we are on the latter, and in the Postmodern era, we are just as confused and frightened by it. Beauty, when it is absent, impacts us considerably. When we walk through an ugly city, we feel the same amount of pain as we do when we walk through a heavily polluted one. In the latter, we cough and sputter; we struggle to breathe. Particles of dust fly into our eyes and soot finds its way under our fingernails. We return to our homes worn and weary with the sense we've just been assailed (and, in a way, we have). So it is with Beauty. When we are surrounded by dankness, when we cast our eyes over a cityscape of wildly mismatched and grotesque architectural forms, we feel similarly harassed—except the traces of this harassment are less palpable. It leaves no soot for us to clean off, no dust for us to wash out. The grime remains buried, not under our fingernails, but in our souls and it never occurs to us to clean it because we don't even know it's there. A similar taint is left on us by ugly music, ugly painting, and ugly literature.

Now, to the relativist I will no doubt seem puritanical. "Beauty is in the eye of the beholder," will be his first rebuff. "The ugly can be also be beautiful," might be his second. But I will say to him, simply, that Beauty is no more in the eye of the beholder than Meaning

[65] The cold, detached protagonist of Robert Musil's modernist masterpiece, *The Man Without Qualities* (1930–1943)

[66] This is a paraphrase. The original reads: "Ulrich asked [Walter] what he really needed a meaning for. One got along alright without it." (*The Man without Qualities*, Volume I, chapter 54)

which is anything but relative. For, of all endeavours that man could conceivably undertake in order to fill his time on earth wisely, there is only a very limited range that can be deemed likely to afford him Meaning: loving, serving others, learning, creating Beauty—to name those proffered by Alain de Botton.[67] All activities not serving one or more of these functions can be confidently judged an unlikely source of Meaning. With the exception of very few individuals, no man could ever content himself to spend the entire span of his adult life working on an industrial production line, devoting all his professional energy to the single act of assembling the same screw over and over again. Such futility precludes Meaning. To argue, as Camus does, that Sisyphus can—or, even worse, *must*—be imagined happy to push a boulder uphill for all eternity, is more absurd than the Absurd itself. Sisyphus needs Meaning almost as urgently as he needs air to breathe. In his daily life, he must be animated by the belief that his actions are not in vain; that they serve a higher purpose. If not, he withers and dies—if not physically, certainly spiritually. We're no different. And since there are comparatively few pursuits that are likely to deliver Meaning and since those few pursuits, when we engage in them effectively, deliver it in abundance, Meaning must be said to be, to a significant extent at least, not a relative, but a fixed ideal.

This same reasoning can be applied to Beauty precisely. As challenging as it may be to accept for those raised on the *Beauty-is-in-the-eye-of-the-beholder* fallacy, sources of Beauty, like sources of meaning, are limited. Just as there are precious few activities that can fill the existential void in someone's life, there are few forms capable of serving as vehicles for the provision of aesthetic satisfaction. A source of Beauty, whether it be a harmoniously designed church façade or an elegantly composed song, strikes the human receptor to which it is directed—the eye, the ear, the mind—with a necessary immediacy that gives the lie even to that other relativist superstition: *even the ugly can be beautiful.* An object, when it is truly beautiful, will make its beauty known with unmitigated power and urgency; producing on

---

[67] Contemporary pop philosopher

the consciousness an impression of such "force and liveliness"[68] as to be deniable only to the most rigorously self-deceiving Postmodernist. When Beauty impresses itself upon the individual, it appeals to her inner emotive being in a way that is completely intuitive and lies well beyond crafty intellectualizations. It can no more be genuinely *logicked* away when it naturally occurs than it can be genuinely *logicked* into existence when it doesn't. It connects and resonates with the individual in that part of her where there are no rational filters and will leave her incapable of accurately expressing it in any other way than by affirming, "This is beautiful." The liveliness and immediacy of this impression is Beauty's litmus test, if you will. Where it is present, there can Beauty be said to lie also. Contrarily, the absence of this lively impression will allow the person space to conjecture of an object that it is "Beautiful in its own way" or "Not my idea of beautiful, but perhaps someone else's"—a luxury that real Beauty never affords. This scenario is Post-modernism's fertile ground; the ideal terrain from which the relativist weed grows and engulfs all that which should remain free of it.

The ugly, too, will make its impression—to be sure. But its force and liveliness will be of an exactly contrary nature. It will leave, not an impression of delight and pleasure as Beauty does, but of pain and disgust. The first will liven the soul; the second will dampen it. The two sensations left by these separate impressions are so clearly distinct from one another, so easily distinguishable that it would take relativist brainwashing of the most thorough kind to rob an individual of his ability to set them apart. And, as unlikely as this kind of brainwashing may seem, our species has proven, over time, all too susceptible to it. To confirm this, you need only look to religious belief and examine how, when firmly held on to, it can hijack the mind, override a person's reason, and make her believe that which

---

[68] This terminology is taken from David Hume's *A Treatise of Human Nature*: "All the perceptions of the human mind resolve themselves into two distinct kinds, which I shall call IMPRESSIONS and IDEAS. The difference betwixt these consists in the degrees of force and liveliness, with which they strike upon the mind, and make their way into our thought or consciousness. Those perceptions, which enter with most force and violence, we may name impressions..." (Book 1, Part 1)

is patently untrue, even in the presence of clear evidence to the contrary, and even when affirming this untruth is tantamount to negating an aspect of one's most fundamental nature.

Let it be heard then: the ugly can no more be beautiful than evil can be good or pain can be pleasant. Only in an age as relativistic as ours could such an affirmation possibly be made without causing uproar.

My critic will no doubt now present me this challenge: *"So, what then are these sources of Beauty you speak of? What is able to deliver Beauty, and how can I distinguish it from that which isn't?"*

This, admittedly, is not an easy question to find an answer for. The definition of Beauty is something philosophers from Plato to Kant have wrestled with over millennia—with arguably inconclusive results. But to say Beauty eludes easy definition is one thing; to say it is nonexistent is another entirely. We may not be able to define happiness or sadness, joy or despondency—not on an irreducible, biochemical level, that is—and yet few of us would question it when we genuinely feel them. Simply because we don't have the means (yet) to determine the precise neurological causes of these sentiments, or the role they play in our lives, it doesn't mean we cannot confirm beyond doubt their reality by recourse to their symptomatic manifestations alone. We may not know from where happiness comes, but when we are overwhelmed by it, we cannot deny it. Similarly, we cannot deny the pleasure afforded by Beauty when it impresses itself upon us, simply because we may not yet be fully equipped to define its essence, its provenance, or the exact role it plays in human affairs.

And even if Beauty were proven not to exist on a strictly conceptual level, this would still not mean much in practical terms. David Hume, a notorious skeptic, argued that true knowledge of cause is impossible. Since our limited sensory organs leave us without the necessary insight to delve deeply into the inner workings of causation, the most we can do is couple cause and effect together chronologically, without ever being able to be completely sure a fundamental nexus between them really exists.[69] This line of skeptical

---

[69] *Enquiry Concerning Human Understanding,* Section 4: Skeptical doubts about the operations of the understanding

reasoning can be applied to Beauty. We may never be able to empirically trace back the pleasure we feel for a beautiful object to its deeper
causes, to the Beauty, in other words, that brings it about, but this
shouldn't stop us from affirming its importance. One day, man may
conceivably invent a philosophical microscope so powerful that it
could, beyond all reasonable doubt, prove that Beauty, as a conceptual entity, never existed at all and could therefore not be claimed to
serve as the causative trigger for the delight we experience at objects
we deem beautiful. But if, in spite of this, we continue, reliably and
without disruption, to feel delight over the same harmonious architectural forms, the same sweetly composed sonnets, the same sumptuous melodies as we have for millennia, what does it even matter?
Could not the Beauty we partake in upon exposure to such stimuli
be said to exist, unequivocally, even if the conceptual entity on which
it is theoretically expected to rest doesn't? And could not this feeling,
if it is consistently felt across individuals across time, be said to be an
entity of its own, able to be treated, studied, applied and recreated, as
if it were a full-fledged, freestanding concept?

I am not unaware of the very real possibility that my critic will
see this last paragraph as a cowardly shirk. "He can't define Beauty,"
he will say, "so he's come up with a clever piece of sophistry to dis-
tract us from it." So I will attempt now to appease him, albeit somewhat clumsily.

Imagine the ugliest architectural forms you've seen and attempt,
for a minute, to extrapolate aesthetic consistencies among them. You
may, if you dwell long and well enough on the subject, come up
with a number of recurring patterns. You might, for example, find
that the truly unpleasant edifice will be either too monotonous in its
design or too varied; either so motivically simple that your eyes are
left unsated and needy for more or so overrun by complexity that,
contrarily, they are burdened and wearied and struggle to make any
sense of it. It may have either too many straight and angular motifs
without enough fluidity to soften them or too many sinuous flourishes without enough linear interruptions there to give those softer
forms relative meaning and impact. It may have not enough colours
or too many. It may be too high in proportion to its width or two

fat in proportion to its height. In all this, an overarching tendency clearly emerges: the tendency toward balance and harmony.

In life as in Art, we live within dichotomous extremes: reason and passion, reality and possibility, chaos and order, the finite and the infinite; existential poles that nature appears to have etched out for us at the dawn of our species. Since, by virtue of how we're hard-wired, we cannot seem to inhabit, for very long, either extreme of these polar relations before being pressed under its weight, we find ourselves swinging, Schopenhauer-style, from one pole to its corresponding contrary, searching for a happy point that falls somewhere in between them. And, though most of us never find it, the burning need for this chimerical balance is never fully lost.

Now an example. The life of the itinerant vagabond and that of the office worker lie at opposite ends of these polar relations—but, in existential terms, they are close equivalents. The vagabond is chaos personified. He lives on the fringes, has no employment, no family or friends. He never knows when or if he'll next eat, where he'll find shelter, nor has anyone to vouch for his safety. He has complete freedom from social responsibility but could die from one minute to the next. The office worker is his exact opposite. He has a home, a job, and loved ones. He has a social welfare and a pension plan. He has all the security in the world, but along with security comes nauseating predictability; his life is largely predetermined, mapped out for him as clearly as if it had already been written on stone tablets. He is rooted in a world of absolute order. Though you may at first feel you know which of these two lives you'd opt for, both are equally unbearable. Give a man chaos without order and, for sure, he'll die the way of the vagabond; alone in a gutter. But grant him the opposite: a perfect utopia in which his every need is provided for and he is want for nothing; a world which is totally secure but is missing that Dostoevskyian *fatal fantastic element*[70]—the thrilling sense that

---

[70] *Notes from Underground,* chapter 8: "Give man everything (economic prosperity) such that he would have nothing to do but to eat, sleep, etc, even then out of sheer ingratitude, sheer spite, man would play you some nasty trick. He would deliberately desire the most fatal rubbish, simply to introduce into all of this good sense, his fatal fantastic element."

his life has not yet revealed all its mystery—and, take it from me, he will be equally miserable. He will die, not once, but every day, repeatedly—of boredom.

The good life is one that straddles the opposing poles of order and chaos. The vagabond never knows if he'll make it through the day and so is chronically fearful, never at rest. The office worker is certain he'll see the morrow. He is secure but has nothing to look forward to and is overwhelmed with ennui. The ideal life is found at a midpoint between these two extremes. It mixes ideal amounts of mystery and certainty, excitement and stability, even suffering and happiness. It affords us assurance of our own identity and safety, but also reassures us that we are not mere "stops in an organ,"[71] life-less puppets in a grotesque vaudeville. It makes us feel safe, yes, but also free. It enables us to extend our wings and fly while assuring us that those wings won't suddenly be clipped off midflight, sending us careening to the ground.

So in Art as in life. In Art, this sweet spot between order and chaos is what might rightly be called Beauty. The beautiful melody, for instance, is one that boasts the ideal combination of long notes and short, slurs and staccatos, small steps and intervallic leaps, soaring peaks and contemplative troughs; one whose harmonic underpinning is neither too static nor too restless. Tweak it slightly in the way of one extreme pole or the other and it's thrown off balance. Repeat one note too many times before moving onto the next, and the melody loses forward thrust and stagnates. Keep its shape entirely stepwise without providing reprieve with a large leap here and there, and it resembles little more than a tedious scale. Here we, as listeners, get bogged down in a predictable hyper-orderedness. And like the office worker, we grow restless and hungry for novelty. But make your melody so syncopated that we can never find the underlying pulse or have it jump about senselessly without repose, and the opposite happens: the melody never settles and it loses itself in

---

71 Borrowed from Dostoevsky's *Notes from Underground*, Chapter 8: "For what is a man without desires, without free will and without choice, if not a stop in an organ?"

its own turmoil. Here we are struck with the fear and anxiety of the vagabond, and perish in chaos, having failed to find structure in the world around us.

So this, then, may furnish a provisional answer to our question. The impression of delight endowed by a work of Art that dexterously walks the tightrope between order and chaos, is, for the moment, as a close to a universal definition of Beauty as I can devise. And, though somewhat inelegant, you might agree it isn't bad at least for a starting point. Even if it doesn't convince you totally, it should be enough to plant the idea that a sound definition of Beauty is not a chimera; that it's well within our intellectual reach. And if Beauty can be defined, then it can also be systematized and systematically achieved in Art. It can be unequivocally recognised when it is embodied and called out when it isn't—without panic, shame, or fear of dogmatic absolutism. A critic who cries ugliness where she sees it is, here, not a pretentious snob holding on to outdated modes of thinking, but a seer of the truth, an upholder and protector of basic, undeniable aspects of our human condition. And an artist who seeks to achieve Beauty in his work is, in turn, not pusillanimous and reactionary, bereft of the skill and courage needed for complete originality, but a medium for the conveyance of a high, noble Truth which his audience will be able to connect with and be ennobled by.

Inspiration

Having devised a workable definition of Beauty in Art, I would like now to set about rebuffing some challenges to my viewpoint I feel will be among the first to come to a critic's mind. The first may be articulated thus: *"If an artist has to abide by your conception of beauty, or any other, wouldn't this undermine the spontaneity of his creative process and take all inspiration out of it, making it dry and formulaic?"*

This would not happen. Even in a world of greater moral and metaphysical certainty, where the values humans lived by were clear and definable, including Beauty, the artist would continue to be an artist and inspiration would continue to play as big a part in his process as it always has. Whenever an artist creates, he always brings to his emerging oeuvre a peculiar and nearly unquantifiable mixture of procedure and intuition. His years of study, learning and practice afford the first, and his natural internal creative spark (also fostered and nurtured by study and learning) accounts for the second. No artist has even created anything of note using just one of these generative impulses to the complete exclusion of the other. Procedure without intuition is dry and formulaic. The contrary, intuition without procedure, is equally if not more undesirable, and can produce nothing more than formless chaos. When Beethoven sat down at his piano and first hammered out the famous opening four notes of his Fifth, he may have done so, initially at least, in the grips of a flash of creative genius, but his subsequent modeling of that germinal material into an entire movement, perfectly structured in every conceivable way, was much belabored. And it could unfold in such a way as to create a flow of interconnected musical ideas so seamless and logically forceful because it was the fruit of years of diligent and effective training in all the major parameters of musical creativity. Beethoven didn't "guess" his way through the composition of that first movement, blindly trusting his inner creative gut. If he'd done this, the movement would have, ironically, turned out sounding the opposite of seamless. His years of repeatedly playing, listening to, and writing music of the highest caliber had refined his inner creative impulse to such a point of rarified sophistication as to have enabled him to concatenate a succession of perfectly interrelated musical ideas, whose unfolding-in-time strikes the ear as logically inevitable, almost as if it had been penned by the hand of nature herself.

To take it a bit further, I can add this: that procedure is a little-understood force; that its reach extends far, much farther than might at first glance be apparent; and that it often steps over into territory usually attributed to intuition. Even where a work may, at first glance, appear so perfect and natural as to have gushed forth freely and entirely from the deepest parts of the artist's inner, intuitive self, there is procedure at work. In fact, quite often, it's when the work seems most intuitively constructed that procedure it most present, even if on a subconscious level. Even the work of a composer like Mozart, traditionally considered an intuitive *par excellence*, who reportedly jotted down great symphonies that were already finished in his mind, as if simply taking down dictation, had a formidable procedural framework built into his inner creative apparatus from an early age, which was so deeply entrenched on a fundamental level that, as it generated the musical structures he would pour into his compositions, it may have taken on all the outward appearance of inspiration while, in actual fact, being the precise opposite. And even those first four notes of Beethoven's Fifth may have appeared to come at him out of the blue, but they too can be argued to have sprung from a wellspring deeper than that. Beethoven "knew" on a subconscious level—a level usually considered intuitive because years of procedural entrenchment have permanently embedded artistic ideas there and rendered them inarticulable—that they would make for a high-octane musical ride. So it's no coincidence that he that of those four, and not any other, appeared to him in that so-called flash of inspiration.

In fact, I might even be able to go so far as to argue convincingly that inspiration is a myth, a word lazily used to give a simplified description to a much more complex creative process—but this is a question for another time.

In both Mozart and Beethoven's day, the values informing sound musical construction were clear and undisputed: formal clarity, logic in motivic development, diatonic tonal order. These values furnished the aesthetic framework that Mozart and Beethoven had internalized on a fundamental level and to which they made appeal continuously, even in moments of so-called inspiration. They worked within a strict conception of artistic beauty that, far from stifling their inspiration, served rather to enhance it, summoning the intuitive spark all great art requires but, at the same time, taming its raw power and shaping it with structure, logic, and clarity.

The Fallacies of Absolute Artistic Freedom and Originality

At this point, my critic may interject: *"Beethoven's symphonies were great, yes, but even he would have created greater masterpieces still, had he been able to enjoy complete artistic freedom, and never had to bother conforming to strict aesthetic and formal values."*

This is the *complete-freedom-is-necessary-to-artistic-expression* fallacy. In a world where individual freedom is exalted above everything else, this stance can seem very appetizing, even self-evident. But I maintain, not only that an artist can still create extraordinary masterpieces within stylistic and aesthetic bounds, even when those bounds are exceedingly narrow, but that this may be, if not the only way, the *best* way to enable him to do so; for, to create work of quality is to create it by conformity to a standard—either perceived or official. Otherwise, it can hardly be imagined how its quality could be reliably evaluated. Without it, the recipient is left to stab in the dark, and can, at most, affirm that a particular work is pleasing to him merely, but might turn out to be quite unappealing to someone else (which is, of course, the relativist's point precisely).

In this sense, relativism is the ultimate artistic shirk. If the Postmodern artist is able to reinvent his art form at will, he also, at the same time, claims the right to reinvent the parameters along which the quality of art is judged. If his art doesn't conform to a standard because he's continually redefining it, then it can't be judged in the way conformant art can, but rather needs to be judged on its own terms. And since in this case there is no fixed set of "terms," for Postmodern Art has successfully liberated itself from any such thing, *"on its own terms"* means, in actual fact, *"on no terms at all,"* and so he's Scott-free. His Art can, at most, be said to be unappealing to the individual merely, but not bad or ugly; not, in other words, unappealing *universally*, according to some immutable ideal.

To ask the artist to create Art by first imposing on herself predetermined stylistic limits within which it must be conceived is to put her to a vital test; exposing herself to the judgment of his audience and critics, who are now armed with the tools they need to judge the quality of his work in definable terms. This is a terrifying prospect indeed, one that many a Postmodern artist hides conveniently behind the relativist fallacy in order to avoid confronting. It will set her another, equally unnerving aesthetic challenge: to channel her creative energies in such a focused manner as to be able maximise the generative potential of said limits, pushing them perhaps here and there, yes, breaking them slightly in the name of creative expression, but remaining largely faithful to them while still contributing something fresh and worthwhile—for it is in this and not in unchecked originality, originality-for-its-own-sake, that the meaning of genius lies.

Here, a related modernist fallacy needs also to be briefly addressed, the fallacy of *absolute originality*. This argues that, in order for an artist to produce work of quality, he needs to be given intellectual freedom such that he will be able to "find his inner creative voice," and liberate it *totally* from the pernicious influences of his contemporaries and idols—for these will only hamper his search for originality and render his work dull and derivative.

For one thing, complete originality of this kind is not possible. We humans are copyists by nature. Every idea we bring forth into this world is either a direct replica of one brought forth already by another before us or an indirect mélange of several ideas already brought forth by several others, which have been combined in our minds without our knowing it. To invent from nothing is a near impossibility. Almost no idea originates in the mind entirely unprompted by external stimulus, but is rather, the product of environmental influence—reworked, possibly, remodeled to suit the purpose at hand, but never manifested from nothingness.

The workings of human language are helpfully analogous. In our daily lives, we utter sentences to express our ideas, using words that were formulated by generations gone by, and applying grammatical constructions we've inherited, not invented. And although the more linguistically ingenious of us may, here and there, coin a neologism or two, most of us will be confined, by and large, to replicating modes of speech that have been handed down to us; that have evolved slowly and incrementally over centuries and millennia to become the highly sophisticated communication systems we know.

So, too, it is with Art. The contemporary artist stands on the shoulders of countless generations of geniuses before him, each having made small but vital contributions to the development of his form. He is bound to draw on this historical legacy, just as we are bound to speak using the past and present tense, and to use the word "dog" to denote man's four-legged friend.

For this reason, absolute originality in Art is a myth. In words attributed to Jim Jarmusch,[72] "Authenticity is invaluable. Originality is nonexistent." That is, the most an artist can aspire to is, not to rid herself of his influences completely, but rather to gather the raw material offered by them and rework it in such a way as to make it her own; to cover up the evident link to its source by putting her own stamp on it.

It will be generally seen, in fact, that the more original an artist appears to be, the more derivative he is. The truly "original" artist tends to have, not less, but more influences than his more derivative peer who draws upon only one or two principle sources of inspiration and, failing to appropriate them well, betrays them instantly. The original artist who knows originality for the lie it is will, not avoid his influences but, on the contrary, lust after them, immerse himself in them and ensure they are as wide and varied as possible, so that when they are combined in his work, they make such a multifarious admixture that their individual origins are all but untraceable. As Picasso allegedly said, "Good artists borrow, great artists steal." This is the closest to originality and the closest to creating great Art that any artist can hope to get: not—as the Modernist would maintain—to reinvent it at every attempt or to hollow it out entirely, but rather to honour the debt he owes to the vast historical legacy on whose shoulders he stands by drawing on it, making it his own and offering, at most, an incremental contribution to it.

Nor, even if complete originality of the kind just rebuffed actually existed, should it necessarily be encouraged. Like language itself, Art is a system for communicating values and ideas. And while it is conceivable that a highly trained linguist may sit in her study for

---

[72] Film director (b. 1953)

months on end and devise her own personal language, replete with an entirely original lexicon, phonological structure, and grammatical system, and while we may applaud her for her efforts, it can hardly be considered advisable for her to go around using it with others and expecting them to comprehend it, much less learn it and speak it themselves. In contemporary Art, such an outlandish approach is, not only acceptable, but generally expected of the artist. The artist/ legislator is expected to reinvent himself with every new opus and, when he fails to do so, he is hounded by the critical establishment. And when his audience fails to understand his new, laboriously elaborated language, they may then and there express their outward admiration for his efforts, but after they've left the gallery or concert hall, they will confess, in hushed and embarrassed tones, their secret bamboozlement.

Art is a language, the language of Beauty, and it is not able to communicate because it has been rendered incomprehensible, it has failed its purpose.

Now I go a step further. Not only is complete creative freedom not a requirement for artistic excellence, it is not even desirable. In his *Poetics of Music* (1947), Stravinsky outlines the dangers to artistic expression posed by having unlimited choices at one's disposal:

> ...at the moment of setting to work and finding myself before the infinitude of possibilities that present themselves, I have the feeling that everything is permissible to me...the best and the worst; if nothing offers me any resistance, then any effort is inconceivable...and consequently every undertaking becomes futile.[73]

In other words, without structure, the artist is aimless—and this is dangerous because, in this aimlessness, all conceivable aesthetic choices appear to be on an equal plane and there is be no way to judge the relative quality of one over the other; no way to evaluate its

---

[73] Chapter 3: "The Composition of Music"

relative potential for being understood by others and ennobling the human spirit. The complete freedom that modern Art vindicates for itself is, not a strength, but the symptom of a malady, which, in his very Nietzschean tendency to warp vice into virtue, the artist refuses to see for what it is. An artistic clime that is purely relativistic is one constituted by a fundamental sense of valuelessness. There is, now, no universal right or wrong, in Art as in life, and we are therefore free in the Sartrian sense—free to make any choice we like. But this freedom comes at a very grave cost.

Stravinsky goes on to describe the limitlessness of creative possibilities he faces as an "abyss":

> Will I then have to lose myself in this abyss of freedom? To what shall I cling in order to escape the dizziness that seizes me before the virtuality of this infinitude?[74]

Stravinsky's choice of words—"abyss" and "dizziness"—is telling indeed. This is the language of Kierkegaard, one of the first philosophers to ever warn of the dangers of complete moral freedom:

> Anxiety (*Angest*) may be compared to dizziness. He whose eye happens to look down into the yawning abyss [of possibilities] becomes dizzy. But what is the reason for this? Anxiety is the dizziness of freedom.[75]

Kierkegaard is especially concerned, here, with the anxiety-provoking prospect of becoming a "self." How does a person come to be who he is? How does one attain one's selfhood? And, here, a brief digression is required.

Kierkegaard believed that, in our innermost selves, we are all a combination of two opposing forces, which he named the "finite"

---

[74] Ibid.
[75] *The Concept of Anxiety* (1844)

and the "infinite": "A human being is a synthesis of the finite and the infinite, of the temporal and the eternal, of freedom and necessity."[76]

The "finite," in this conception, is the sum total of all that which by necessity defines or limits us; all aspects of our being that we can't change, including our place and date of birth, who our biological mother and father are, the fact that we're human, of a certain height, hair and eye colour. The "infinite" is the opposite and encompasses all the things that aren't permanent fixtures of our essence; all that which we can, if we really want to, alter, remove or rise above: an unhealthy belief, a soulless office job, our unhappy marriage. In searching for our selfhood, Kierkegaard argues that many of us make the first of two fundamental errors: we get bogged down in the finite. We assume that there's more to us that's fixed and unalterable than there actually is and end up putting up with it needlessly.[77] We stay in that awful job, or that loveless marriage, we continue believing that comfortable untruth that doesn't serve us. We blindly follow the herd and, in doing so, negate ourselves and fall into "despair."[78]

But there is a second, contrary error which is perhaps less common but equally perilous: to spend one's life entirely in the realm of the "infinite," endlessly searching for one's selfhood, shifting from one "self" to another but never actually settling on one; ending up thus overwhelmed by the "dizziness" and, finally, drowning in the "abyss."[79]

---

[76] *Sickness unto Death* (1849), Part One, A: *The Sickness unto Death is Despair*

[77] *Sickness unto Death*, Part One, C: "Such a person forgets himself…forgets his own name, dares not believe in himself, finds being himself too risky, finds it much easier and safer to like the others, to become a copy, a number, along with the crowd."

[78] For Kierkegaard, "despair" was a sickness of the spirit; the sickness of losing oneself, of not knowing one's inner essence. See *Sickness unto Death*, Part One, A: "Despair is the imbalance in a relation of synthesis, in a relation which relates to itself."

[79] Ibid: "Now if possibility outstrips necessity, the self runs away from itself in possibility so that it has no necessity to return to. This, then, is possibility's despair. Here the self becomes an abstract possibility; it exhausts itself floundering about in possibility."

However thrilling a prospect may at first appear to us, complete freedom is the opposite of liberating; it is, in fact, profoundly debilitating. It leaves us languishing, in a world where nothing is certain and we struggle to make sense of everything, especially ourselves. So it is in Art as well as in life. An artist who drifts endlessly is an artist who is drowning in an abyss of relativist valuelessness, in a world where there is no right or wrong, just choices. And if she can't save herself from perishing in Kierkegaard's infinite, if she remains adrift forever, so too will the Art she is meant to be developing.

And besides everything already discussed, this must also be said: if you make an artist believe he has complete freedom, he'll turn that freedom on himself and on others. Alongside the beautiful and the ennobling, he'll also create the base, the ignoble, the ugly. Though he may one day decorate your wall with a masterful canvas, the next, if whim gets the better of him, he will just as likely place a tin of his own excrement in your living room[80] and insist it is equally worthy of your appreciation. The artist is a pesky rebel by nature, more so even than the layman, who himself is no cipher. And if he's not tamed, he'll take the unqualified freedom you're foolish enough to grant him and use it as a stick with which to beat you over the head.

A Civilizational Quarter-Life Crisis

A further concern of my critic might be the following: *"Would you suggest that all Art that doesn't conform to your standard of Beauty be discarded? Expelled from the canon forever?"*

This would be pointless. And it would needlessly rid the world of a great number of sublime works. Modernist masterpieces like Stravinsky's *Rite of Spring,* Joyce's *Ulysses,* and Munch's *Scream* would not qualify as Beautiful under my definition. These three works, all of them, teeter far, too far over the edge of the chasm of chaos, and

---

[80] This is reference to a work by artist Piero Manzoni called *Merda d'artista* or *Artist's Shit* (1961), in which he allegedly filled ninety tin cans with his own excrement.

in some cases, fall precipitously into it—*The Rite,* because it's a tour de force of rhythmic instability and unresolved harmonic dissonance; *The Scream,* because its very purpose is to embody, with unapologetic commitment, that which is ugly; and *Ulysses,* because it takes it upon itself to stretch the boundaries of language and the conventions of literary expression to their very breaking points. But without these, we would, as a civilisation, be all the poorer, bereft of hugely important artistic chronicles of times gone by and the sentiments that characterised by them. While not necessarily beautiful, they are far from worthless (and by the by, I never said Art needed to be beautiful in order to be worthwhile; it simply is more worthwhile if it is). These three works are relevant because they are supreme illustrators of the aesthetic temperament and moral ambivalence of their time and no other works in their place could conceivably have better captured these with greater accuracy. I would no more suggest to do away with *The Rite* than I would to do away with the human emotions it captures: shock, horror, confusion, anguish, and fear; but also resilience, boldness, and defiance. These are sentiments necessary for the well-roundedness of any individual and, in times of crisis, perfectly natural and beneficial for him to experience for they serve as vital vehicles toward growth and self-regeneration.

So too on a collective level, a civilization undergoing a crisis of identity would quite naturally be expected to feel a shared fear and confusion, which in turn would sublimate themselves in an aesthetic of stylistic waywardness, continuous self-questioning, and crippling self-doubt. If Stravinsky, Schönberg, and Boulez buried traditional Western music, and now, the likes of Philip Glass and Schnittke are standing over the grave, dancing before the tombstone, we can hardly be surprised, given the historical framework within which they have all lived and worked. It's hardly conceivable for an artist to hold on to a sense of aesthetic clarity that the prevailing metaphysical and moral uncertainty doesn't allow. An artist's job is, not to deny the spirit of his age, but to capture it. And he cannot capture, in art, metaphysical sturdiness afforded by an absolute value system, when his ask is rather to chronicle the angst brought about by its collapse.

So no, I'm not calling for a discard of all art created under the banner of modernist experimentalism or even of Postmodern relativism. What I am trying to do, however, is to urge the reader to see it, not for what it purports to be, but for what it actually is: not the affirmation of a collective spirit brimming with confidence nor the proud fanfare of a healthy and robust aesthetic that's certain of what it is; but rather, a cry of anguish from a troubled, confused and ailing civilization, still reeling from the collapse of its godly order and struggling desperately to find meaning in its aftermath. Judged from this perspective, the historical significance of the Postmodern value system becomes quite clear. It is not a set of noble virtues promoting freedom of expression and creative diversity, but rather an unfortunate temporary byproduct of rampant civilizational confusion and directionlessness; an aesthetic we need to not defend and uphold, but nurse and overcome as we might a psychiatric disorder—or we risk staying in its grips for longer than we need to.

Toward a New Beauty

Eager to get to the crux of the discussion, my especially ambitious critic may now raise the following, legitimate query: *"The Beauty (and metaphysic) of epochs gone by was god-derived, and collapsed when god was declared 'dead.' You're not suggesting we resurrect god, are you?"*

My answer to this is simple and clear. I would no more suggest we return to the Abrahamic god simply to enjoy the metaphysical certainty he afforded than I would we re-embrace the pagan beliefs popular before his advent—or any other false belief system. This would be patently absurd. I agree that, as a species, we can and must progress beyond the collective psychopathology of religious dogma. The collapse of the old moral order was a painful but necessary step in our evolution and, to this day, the philosophical fallout it's caused is strongly felt. But to suggest we return to it simply in order to soothe the pain its removal has caused would be akin to suggesting that a recovering addict take heroin to soothe his withdrawals. Collective metaphysical and moral certainty seems, to me, to be vital for the spiritual health of a civilization; it provides a structure within which shared consciousness can navigate and thrive. If a social unit knows upon what values it is founded, then it knows what collective goals it should aspire to and propel itself toward. If not, it is aimless and remains forever adrift in Kierkegaard's infinite.

Not satisfied, my critic might now add: *"What value system are you suggesting we adopt then, if not god's? All human-derived metaphysical and ethical codes are arbitrary, incapable of affording the certainty you feel we need."*

When I hear this objection, I'm reminded once again of Ivan's famous nihilistic proclamation in *The Brothers Karamazov*: "If God doesn't exist, all is permitted." In a godless universe, where there is no divine authority mandating good and evil—the reasoning goes— there can be no universal values, no fixed morality for all moral prescriptions imposed by man can just as easily be undone by him. This can at first seem very persuasive—and terrifying. It calls to mind visions of a nightmarish dystopia in which individualist whim has run amok and everyone allows himself the freedom to act as he pleases, a hellish reality not too dissimilar from the Hobbesian state of "*bellum omnium contra omnes.*"[81] But though this may have been a valid apprehension for a hundred or so years, one that philosophers from Nietzsche to Sartre felt the need to wrestle with, I believe it's now high time we cast it aside.

The idea that the only appropriate philosophical response to the question of godlessness is nihilism is outdated and wrong. The rather unflattering assumption that seems to underpin it is this: that we are, by nature, helplessly feeble and overwhelmingly susceptible to our baser, darker impulses.

This was the rather pessimistic view of Freud who, in his *Civilisation and its Discontents* (1930), argued the following:

---

[81] "A war of all against all," a concept Thomas Hobbes introduces in his *De Cive* (1642) and explores again in his *Leviathan* (1651), in a chapter entitled "On the natural condition of mankind as concerning their felicity, and misery" (p. 83).

The bit of truth behind all this—one so eagerly denied—is that men are not gentle, friendly creatures wishing for love who simply defend themselves if they are attacked, but that a powerful measure of desire for aggression has to be reckoned as part of their instinctual endowment. The result is that their neighbour is to them not only a possible helper or sexual object, but also a temptation to them to gratify their aggressiveness on him, to exploit his capacity for work without recompense, to use him sexually without his consent, to seize his possessions, to humiliate him, to cause him pain, to torture and kill him.[82]

Man, for Freud, was "*Homo homini lupus*" or his very own man-eating wolf.[83] And who would dare deny it in the face of indisputable historical evidence; all the atrocities we've committed over the millennia, all the wars we've waged, all the blood that's been spilt?

It is a rather grim picture of humanity, one in which our nobler faculties—our reason, intellect, love and compassion, our thirst for knowledge, our drive to self-betterment and self-understanding (all aspects of the human inner world just as engrained and prominent as their baser counterparts)—seem not to figure at all. It seems to overlook the fact that, for every inquisition we've launched, we've penned dozens of symphonies and novels; for every life we've lost on the battlefield, we've saved hundreds in medical laboratories; for every act of savagery committed in ignorance, countless have been prevented by increased learning and education. In subscribing to it, one could quite easily conclude that we are so helplessly susceptible to evil, that the only way can withstand it, is if we place an omnipotent castigator between it and us; an impenetrable cosmic barrier without which our

---

[82] Location 830
[83] Ibid., location 838

primitive impulses to egoism, uncontrolled sexual indulgence, hostility, and aggression would very quickly take hold and overrun us.

But this is not the case at all. A very simple thought-game that gives the lie to the fallacy of ultimate moral reliance on god is one you can perform with very little effort. Think of the last time you entertained the idea of doing another person harm and ask yourself if it was either the disconformity of that contemplated act to divine command or the fear of divine punishment that might have resulted from its execution that finally stopped you from you from carrying it out. If your answer is "no," as I wager it will be, then you might also be able to offer alternative explanations for your restraint. Perhaps it was empathy for the other person's suffering or fear of their judgment or of society's. Perhaps it was the sense of guilt you anticipated would rack you afterwards. Or it might have been simply the idea that it was humanly (not cosmically) wrong; that, if everyone went around committing misdemeanours like the one you contemplated, the world would be a slightly darker place for it.

This last consideration, in fact, is one that Immanuel Kant lay at the foundation of his *Categorical Imperative*, a formula he set forth for evaluating the moral viability of a hypothetical behavior—or, as he called it, a *maxim*. It goes like this: "I am never to act otherwise than so that I could also will that my maxim should become a universal law."[84]

Or rendered more accessibly: before I carry out a morally ambivalent action, I must first imagine a world in which this action was carried out by all people at all times and ask myself if this is the kind of world I'd like to live in. If it isn't, then I should refrain from it. Kant uses the example of a promise made without the sincere intention of keeping it:

The shortest way…and an unerring one, to discover the answer to this question whether a lying promise is consistent with duty, is to ask myself, "Should I be content that my maxim…should hold good as a universal law… Then I presently become aware that while I can

---

[84] *Groundwork for the Metaphysics of Morals* (1785), First Section: Transition from the Common Rational Knowledge of Morality to the Philosophical

will the lie, I can by no means will that lying should be a universal law. For with such a law there would be no promises at all, since it would be in vain to allege my intention in regard to my future actions to those who would not believe this allegation…"[85]

In other words, the next time you entertain making someone a false promise, think about what would happen if everyone made false promises all the time. In such a world, no one would ever trust anyone and you wouldn't be able to get away the false promise to begin with. Ergo the maxim nullifies itself and cannot be considered universally good.

Kant was one of the greatest ethical philosophers of the eighteenth century. And, though not irreligious in the strict sense of the term, he was in a very important way a product of the enlightened ideals of his time: in his exultation of Reason. Like most of his colleagues of the 1600s and 1700s—from Descartes to Rousseau, from Locke to Hume—his ethical preoccupation was to find an alternative font to god and divine *Logos* for a solid human metaphysical superstructure. His categorical imperative is, thus, profoundly human-centred. It suggests that, in our quest for the universal right and wrong, we need make appeal to no more abstract and remote a legislative power than our thinking, logicking minds. We can arrive at a sound principle of good ethics, as Kant puts it, "without quitting the moral knowledge of common human reason."[86] No divine authority is needed nor any commandment or holy book.

The categorical imperative may not be without its practical glitches. For starters, it relies on an absurd proposition for its persuasive force: the absolute ubiquity of an extremely specific behavior. You might rightly ask yourself why you should bother conjuring up, in your imagination, a hypothetical dystopian scenario that is not even remotely likely to ever manifest itself in reality and then direct your behavior on the basis of it. You might also question Kant's overestimation of humanity's innate ethical uniformity. In any given scenario, while you may be strongly inclined toward one moral outcome,

---

[85] Ibid.
[86] Ibid.

I could very conceivably prefer another, quite different one. And if all you're able to do is evaluate the rectitude of your behavior using your own personal internal compass, then in spite of your best intentions, you may end up doing wrong by me while all along believing quite earnestly that you're doing the opposite. Individual variations stemming from differences in temperament, cultural milieu, and socio-economic background are admittedly not unremarkable. But Kant's thought experiment does, I believe, suggest one important way in which we are universally the same: in our very real ability to temper the baser aspects of our natures with the nobler; to counteract our vices with our virtues; to wield our human reason to combat our animal egoism. And if we have this, we have all the tools we need to devise morality within human bounds alone.

Recent contributions to evolutionary theory have added biological reinforcement to this idea. Evolutionary psychologists like Robert Wright have taken it upon themselves to prove that our moral systems are largely the product, not of cultural variation between one people and another, but of the collective genetic history of our species and are, therefore, much less arbitrary and more uniform than has traditionally been assumed. In his *The Moral Animal* (1994), Wright argues that almost all human values have a solid genetic basis.[87] These include empathy, compassion, altruism—but even more complex ethical microsystems, like social justice, class hierarchy, friendship, and romantic love, which were traditionally claimed by the cultural determinists to be context-dependent. We are guided, morally, by Darwinian forces, with the most radical behavioural differences among people wholly accountable as tailored responses of the same underlying genetic procedure to environmental differences.[88] All this suggests that morality is not a free act of human intellectual creativity. To an extent greater than usually assumed, morality is mapped out for us by our genes, and our functional ethical mandates—both social and legal—tend often to be real-life manifestations of deeply entrenched and genetically encoded inclinations.

---

[87] Introduction: Darwin and us
[88] Ibid.

Here a likely misunderstanding must at once be averted. We may be predisposed, by nature, toward certain behaviours, but this doesn't mean we're obliged to live by them unquestioningly. And this is just as well, for evolution may have endowed us with altruism and compassion, but it's also burdened us with egoism, hatred, and intolerance. We may be tempted to assert that, in accepting natural morality, can't take on the first set of values without at the same time getting the second as an unwanted byproduct. But this would be tantamount to falling into a well-known philosophical trap: the *"appeal to nature"* fallacy, according to which all that is natural is necessarily good. A base and problematic human attribute, like intolerance, one more likely to breed strife than harmony, is still base even though it may have come to us through the processes of natural selection.

Evolution doesn't write moral law. It guides it. To argue that, when we recognise nature as a guiding force in human morality, we must accept it warts and all, is to endow it with a legislative omnipotence, an irresistibly prescriptive force it doesn't, per sé, possess.

Nature may partly yield morality, but it is itself amoral and works its effect with, at most, a passing care for social harmony, the common good, and personal fulfillment. "Natural selection never promised us a rose garden," Wright says. "It doesn't 'want' us to be happy. It 'wants' us to be genetically prolific."[89] This affirmation, though undeniably Schopenhauerian in its bleakness, shouldn't depress us too much; it should, rather, empower us. Armed with the knowledge of our genetic shortcomings, we have all the tools we need for exponential collective self-improvement. We can retain the nobler aspects of our nature and wield them to the fulfillment of our collective goals, while at the same time, recognising our baser traits for what they are and mitigating them with our higher ones, so that they don't impede it.

What evolutionary theory does well is furnish us with a paradigm within which we can come to a deeper, more informed understanding of ourselves, our emotions, our impulses and instincts. It gives an insight into how nature sculpts our proclivity for certain

---

[89] Chapter 10: Darwin's Conscience

behaviours and our disinclination from others. What it doesn't do is dictate the moral significance we should then attribute to these. This, I would argue, is ours to decide based on values we willingly adopt. And any value we employ as an overarching guiding principle in our moral system should be chosen for its aptitude at supplementing natural morality, filling its gaps and straightening its kinks. If nature proves insufficient at suppressing hatred and bigotry, we must counteract it with mandates to love, empathy, and compassion. If it proves inept at maintaining individual and collective happiness, we must redirect it to minimise suffering and maximise wellbeing; to serve the common good; to provide us, as people and as a species, with readily accessible fonts of meaning and purpose.

All this should give us great hope. Having devised a sober, human-centred morality, suited to the modern spirit and free both of godly superstition and nihilistic reductions, future generations will be equipped with all the tools they need to rebuild a metaphysic and, therefore, a Beauty for the modern age. For, as hope has been made more than evident thus far, Beauty is nothing if not the manifestation, through art, of all that is considered ethically and metaphysically good.

Dedicated to my beloved Papà, to whom
I owe everything. RIP, Amico Fritz.

Bibliography

Alighieri, Dante. *The Divine Comedy: Inferno.* Tr. John Ciardi. New York: New American Library, 1954.

Alighieri, Dante. *The Divine Comedy: Paradiso.* Tr. John Ciardi. New York: New American Library, 1961.

Alighieri, Dante. *The Divine Comedy: Purgatorio.* Tr. John Ciardi. New York: New American Library, 1961.

Aquinas, Thomas. *Summa contra Gentiles.* Tr. Anton C. Pegis. Notre Dame, Indiana: Double Day & Company, Inc., 2014.

Aquinas, Thomas. *Summa Theologica. Summa Theologica.* e-artnow, 2013.

Augustine, St. *The City of God.* Tr. Marcus Dods. New York: Modern Library Classics, 2000.

Burckhardt, Jakob. *The Civilisation of the Renaissance in Italy.* Tr. S. C. G.

Middlemore. New York: Penguin Classics, 1990.

Camus, Albert. *The Myth of Sisyphus.* New York: Vintage International (2nd ed.), 2018.

Descartes, René. *Discourse on the Method and Meditations on First Philosophy.*

Indianapolis/Cambridge: Hackett Publishing Company (4th ed.), 1998.

Dostoevsky, Fyodor. *The Brothers Karamazov.* Tr. Ignat Avsey. Oxford: Oxford University Press, 1994.

Dostoevsky, Fyodor. *Notes from Underground and the Double.* Tr. Ronald Wilks. New York: Penguin Classics, 2009.

Fichte, Johann G. *The Science of Knowledge*. Tr. Peter Heath and John Lachs.
Cambridge: Cambridge University Press, 1982.

Freud, Sigmund. *Civilisation and its Discontents*. Tr. David McLintock. New York: Penguin Classics, 2002.

Hegel, Georg W. F. *The Phenomenology of Spirit*. Tr. Peter Fuss and John Dobbins. Notre Dame, Indiana: University of Notre Dame, 2019.

Hobbes, Thomas. *Leviathan*. Oxford: Oxford University Press, 1996.

Hume, David. *An Inquiry Concerning Human Understanding*. Indianapolis/Cambridge: Hackett Publishing Company (2nd ed.), 1993.

Hume, David. *A Treatise on Human Nature*. New York: Penguin Classics, 1985.

Kant, Immanuel. *Groundwork of the Metaphysics of Morals*. Tr. Mary Gregor et al. Cambridge. Cambridge University Press (2nd ed.), 2012.

Kant, Immanuel. *A Critique of Pure Reason*. Tr. Thomas Kingsmill Abbott. Digi Reads, 2017.

Kierkegaard, Søren. *The Concept of Anxiety*. Tr. Alastair Hannay. New York: Liverlight Paperback, 2015.

Kierkegaard, Søren. *Either/Or: A fragment of life*. Tr. Alastair Hannay. New York: Penguin Classics (Revised ed.), 1992.

Kierkegaard, Søren. *Sickness unto Death*. Tr. Alastair Hannay. New York: Penguin Classics, 1989.

Kramer, Hilton. *The Triumph of Modernism*. Roman & Littlefield: Lanham, Maryland, 2013.

Locke, John. *Essay Concerning Human Understanding*. Ware, Hertfordshire: Wordsworth Editions Ltd., 2014.

Locke, John. *The Second Treatise of Government*. Cambridge: Cambridge University Press, 1988.

Lyotard, Jean-François. *The Postmodern Condition*. Manchester: Manchester University Press, 1997.

Mirandola, Pico della. *Oration on the Dignity of Man*. New York: Cambridge University Press, 2012.

Musil, Robert. *The Man without Qualities,* Vol. 1. Tr. Sophie Wilkins and Burton Pike. New York: Vintage Publishing, 1996.

Nietzsche, Friedrich. *Thus Spoke Zarathustra.* Tr. R. J. Hollingdale. New York: Penguin Classics, 1961.

Petrarch, Francesco. *Il Canzoniere.* Tr. Mark Musa with Barbara Manfredi. Bloomington & Indianapolis: Indiana University Press, 1996.

Petrarch, Francesco. *Coronation Oration.* JSTOR. Ernest H. Wilkins. 09.09.2020. https://www.jstor.org/stable/460017?seq=10#metadata_info_tab_contents.

Rousseau, Jacques. *The Social Contract.* Tr. H.J. Tozer. Ware, Hertfordshire: Wordsworth Editions Ltd., 1998.

Russell, Bertrand. *A History of Western Philosophy.* London: Routledge Classics, 2004.

Schelling, Friedrich W. J. *Philosophical Investigations into the Essence of Human Freedom.* Tr. Jeff Love and Johannes Schmidt. Albany: State University of New York Press, 2006.

Stravinsky, Igor: *The Poetics of Music.* Cambridge, Massachusetts: Harvard University Press (Revised ed.), 1970.

Wright, Robert. *The Moral Animal.* New York: Vintage Publishing (Reprint ed.), 2010.

About the Author

Ilario Colli is an Australian-born author, thinker, and arts journalist. At the University of Western Australia, he received two degrees, in arts and in music, as well as several academic awards. It has been said of him: "Ilario ought rightly to be considered Australia's 'finest classical music writer.'" He has written extensively for *Limelight Magazine*, Australia's foremost arts publication, for which he interviewed such greats as Ennio Morricone and David Helfgott. He contributes regularly to his own blog site: www.thoughtgymnasium. com. He now lives in New York City. He's completing Postgraduate studies at the New School, where he was the recipient of the Provost scholarship. *In Art As in Life* is his first major published work.

CPSIA information can be obtained
at www.ICGtesting.com
Printed in the USA
FSHW012000070721
82910FS